"It is a relief to find a book on the life of faith that is honest about the pain of emptiness and the fear of losing all that orients your life. Nothing glib here and nothing super-human: just putting one foot in front of the other with whatever trust you can manage, because there is no other way to go."

—Dr. Rowan Williams, Archbishop of Canterbury

"Halfway through *Still* I realized that a lot of spiritual books—most, maybe—are written during a mid-faith crisis. Too few admit it. But Winner grabs God's hidden-ness by the shoulders and will not let go. She knows the grace that can only be learned when we stand with Moses, staring into the raging waters, and hear a voice say, 'The LORD will fight for you; you need only to stand still.'"

— Jonathan Wilson-Hartgrove, author of
The Wisdom of Stability

"Still water reveals depth—as does this account of ordinary life and what lies beneath."

—Philip Yancey, author of *What Good Is God?*

"An unusually painful story, told with rare honesty by an unusually gifted writer."

—N. T. Wright, author of *Simply Jesus*

"It takes courage to put your soul through an X-ray and let the world see the breaks, the tears, the strains, the scars. Still, this is my favorite of her books yet."

—Brian McLaren, author of *Naked Spirituality: A Life with God in 12 Simple Words*

"A courageous tour into the murky darkness of . . . a faith unraveling before our eyes. *Still* persists into a gentle version of the gospel."

—Scot McKnight, Karl A. Olsson Professor in Religious Studies at North Park University

PRAISE FOR *Girl Meets God*

"Winner is insatiable, and dauntless, in her search for religious truth, at whatever personal cost. The sheer energy of her quest, combined with refreshing honesty and flashes of wild humor, give her story its edge."

—*New York Times*

"Winner seems to possess a passionate, if somewhat promiscuous, religious sensibility. . . . [She] shows a sure sense of what ritual and religious community can mean and a compelling ability to make Scripture come alive."

—*Chicago Tribune*

Still

Still NOTES ON A MID-FAITH CRISIS

lauren f. winner

HarperOne
An Imprint of HarperCollinsPublishers

HarperOne

STILL: *Notes on a Mid-Faith Crisis.* Copyright © 2012 by Lauren F. Winner. All rights reserved. Printed in the United States of America. No part of this book may be used or reproduced in any manner whatsoever without written permission except in the case of brief quotations embodied in critical articles and reviews. For information address HarperCollins Publishers, 10 East 53rd Street, New York, NY 10022.

HarperCollins books may be purchased for educational, business, or sales promotional use. For information please write: Special Markets Department, HarperCollins Publishers, 10 East 53rd Street, New York, NY 10022.

HarperCollins website: http://www.harpercollins.com

HarperCollins®, 📖®, and HarperOne™ are trademarks of HarperCollins Publishers.

FIRST EDITION

Library of Congress Cataloging-in-Publication Data
Winner, Lauren F.
Still : notes on a mid-faith crisis / Lauren F. Winner.—1st ed.
p. cm.
ISBN 978–0–06–176811–8
1. Winner, Lauren F. 2. Christian life—Anglican authors. 3. Anglican converts—United States—Biography. 4. Christian converts from Judaism—United States—Biography. I. Title.
BV2623.W56A3 2012
283.092—dc23
[B]   2011017200

12 13 14 15 16   RRD(H)   10 9 8 7 6 5 4 3 2 1

This book is dedicated to Lil Copan,
with thankfulness for her friendship,
her wisdom, and her abiding

He wonders if he's lying. If he is, he is hung
in the middle of nowhere, and the thought
hollows him.

—*John Updike*

preface

Jane Smiley's novel *Horse Heaven* was published in 2000,
about three years after I left the Judaism in which I had
grown up and was baptized in the Anglican church.
Smiley is quite possibly my favorite living American
novelist—I read her novella "The Age of Grief" at least
once annually—and I snatched up *Horse Heaven* as soon
as it hit the stands. It's a sprawling comic novel about
horse racing, a subculture I have little interest in, and it
is not my favorite of the Smiley oeuvre: I prefer her quiet,
finely grained family stories—*Ordinary Love and Good
Will, Barn Blind, At Paradise Gate*. But one small section
of *Horse Heaven* spoke to me with a force I had mostly
felt only when reading liturgy or poetry or epitaphs. Here,

Smiley is writing about a horse trainer named Buddy Crawford. He gets born again and he's all fired up and then one night he is praying and he sits down on the bed and he looks "up to the full moon, in whose region he imagines Jesus to be," and then he begins to talk to his Lord and Savior. "Okay. Here's the deal," Buddy Crawford says. "I thought I was saved. That was what was advertised. I would accept you as my personal savior, and there you were. And, you know, I felt it, too. I felt saved and everything. . . . But I find out all the time that I've got to keep getting saved. Am I saved? Am I not saved? What do I do now? . . . Are you talking to me? Are you not talking to me? Am I good? Am I a sinner? Still a sinner?" And then he bursts into tears.

His wife comes into the room, gets undressed, and asks Buddy what has made him cry. "When the Lord came into me," Buddy tells her, "it was such a good feeling, I thought, Well, I can do anything because of this feeling, but then there was all this stuff to do and to think about, and I don't remember the feeling all that well."

It seemed to me that I was reading my own tea leaves when I read those Jane Smiley words. I had not yet had any such experience, any shaking failure of memory, any overpowering uncertainty about whether anything I thought I believed about God was actually true. I was still secure in the grip of certainties, many of them: that Jesus was real, that he was God, that he had come to me in a dream; that God was intimately involved with the particulars of my life; that my days would and should revolve around the institution where people went to meet and get to know and worship this Jesus, that is, the church; that God had saved me; that God was saving me still.

But lying there reading Jane Smiley's fiction on the hand-me-down futon in my small grad-school garret in Manhattan's Morningside Heights—I recall that I was drinking cherry-flavored sparkling water as I read, that the water was room temperature but the bubbles felt cold on my throat—I knew that one day, I would sit by Buddy Crawford's side.

This is a book about what happens when you come to your Buddy Crawford moment, and then what happens after that.

~

I have never used Crawford's language of the Lord coming into me. If you asked me how I came to Christianity, I would tell you about my childhood—about growing up with a Jewish father and a lapsed Baptist mother who had agreed to raise my sister and me as Jews; about how I loved Judaism, the synagogue, the Jewish meditation group I attended every month. I would tell you about baking challah and singing songs by Debbie Friedman and how I loved each letter of the Hebrew alphabet. And then I would tell you that when I was in college, unexpected things happened: I had this dream about Jesus rescuing me from a kidnapping; and I obsessively read Jan Karon's Mitford novels, whose protagonist is an Episcopal priest and whose many characters are always quoting the Bible, sensing Jesus' nearness, trusting him; and I bought a Book of Common Prayer and started using it to guide my conversations with God; and then finally, I graduated from college and moved to England, and there I was baptized. I would tell you how unexpected this was, how I never expected Christianity—but also how absorbed I became in this new faith, how wholehearted my embrace of it. I was just about the most enthusiastic new Christian you had ever met—in church all the time, reading about church things when I was not at church, wanting nothing more than prayer, Communion, hymns.

I know there must have been feelings in the midst of the kidnapping dream and the prayer book purchase. I suspect they were feelings of closeness, maybe of rest, of an intense knowing and being known by God—but I'm just guessing. Like Buddy Crawford, I don't remember the feelings very well. Actually, I don't remember them at all.

Am I saved? Am I not saved? Are you talking to me? Are you not talking to me? Am I a sinner? Still a sinner? What do I do now?

What happens in conversion—at least, what happened in mine—is that a person concludes that the truth is in Jesus. That conclusion will carry you to baptism; it will carry you to church, or back to church, or to your knees. But then where does it take you? Or, more precisely, how does it take you? How do you continue to allow the truth that is in Jesus to be your rudder?

The kidnapping dream and the prayer book and the baptism made a path; they were my glory road, and I thought that road would carry me forever. I didn't anticipate that, some years in, it would carry me to a blank wall, and at that wall a series of questions: do I just stand here staring at this wall? Do I go over? Under? Do I turn around and retrace my steps?

The enthusiasms of my conversion have worn off. For whole stretches since the dream, since the baptism, my belief has faltered, my sense of God's closeness has grown strained, my efforts at living in accord with what I take to be the call of the gospel have come undone.

And yet in those same moments of strained belief, of not knowing where or if God is, it has also seemed that the Christian story keeps explaining who and where I am, better than any other story I know. On the days when I think I have a fighting chance at redemption, at change, I understand it to be these words and these rituals and these people who will change me. Some days I am not sure if my faith is riddled with doubt or whether, graciously, my doubt is riddled with faith. And yet I continue to live in a world the way a religious person lives in the world; I keep living in a world that I know to be enchanted, and not left alone. I doubt; I am uncertain; I am restless, prone to wander. And yet glimmers of holy keep interrupting my gaze.

In the American church, we have a long tradition of telling spiritual stories that culminate in conversion, in the narrator's joining the church, getting dunked in the waters of baptism, getting saved. But what Buddy Crawford knows is that the baptism, the conversion, is just the beginning, and what follows is a middle, and the middle may be long, and it may have little to do with whatever it was that got you to the font.

This is a book about entering the middle, about being in the middle of the spiritual life.

～

I was carried to the middle of my spiritual life by two particular events: my mother died, and I got married, and the marriage was an unhappy one. Had you asked me

before—before my mother got sick, before I found myself
to be a person thinking about divorce—I would have told
you that these were precisely the circumstances in which
one would be glad for religious faith. Faith, after all, is
supposed to sustain you through hard times—and I'm
sure for many people faith does just that. But it wasn't so
for me. In my case, as everything else was dying, my faith
seemed to die, too. God had been there. God had been
alive to me. And then, it seemed, nothing was alive—not
even God.

Intuition and conversation persuade me that most of
us arrive at a spiritual middle, probably we arrive at many
middles, and there are many ways to get there. The events
that brought me to the middle of my spiritual life were
dramatic, they were interruptions, they were grief.

But grief and failure and drama are not the only paths
to a spiritual middle. Sometimes a whole life of straightforward churchgoing takes you to a middle. Sometimes it
is not about a conversion giving way, or the shock of God's
absence. Sometimes a life of wandering takes you to a
middle. Sometimes you come to the middle quietly.

You may arrive at the spiritual middle exhausted, in
agony, in what saints of the Christian tradition have called
desolation.

Or your journey to the middle may be a little easier, a

little calmer—it is not that God is absent—it is, rather, that your spiritual life seems to have faded, like fabric. Some days the fading doesn't trouble you at all; other days, it seems a hollowing loss. You're not as interested as you once were in attending to God. You no longer find it easy to make time for church, for prayer.

Whether you feel a wrenching anguish or simply a kind of distracted listlessness, the middle looks unfamiliar when you get there. The assumptions and habits that sustained you in your faith life in earlier years no longer seem to hold you. A God who was once close seems somehow farther away, maybe in hiding.

This book is not a manual for "getting through" the middle—I don't think the middle is something to be gotten through, and I don't have instructions, in any event.

Nor is it an apologetics—a defense of Christianity, offered as a rejoinder to my own questions and hesitations; or, if it is an apologetics, it is an apologetics only for continuing to abide in faith amid uncertainties, in the interstices of belief.

Nor is *Still* a memoir, although it is set in an autobiographical frame and you will encounter some of the particulars of my own middle moment.

Rather, this book is about the time when the things you thought you knew about the spiritual life turn out not to

suffice for the life you are actually living. This book wants
to know about that time, and then about the new ways
you find, the new glory road that might not be a glory road
after all but just an ordinary gravel byway, studded with
the occasional bluet, the occasional mica chip.

I have organized the chapters into three sections. In the
first section, I am at the wall. I have been standing at this
wall a long time. God is absent; perhaps I am absent from
myself. The conversion is over. Everything has changed,
everything needs to change. But what is the change? How
to change?

The second section is a picture of wrestling with a God
who isn't there, or maybe who is: what do you do in the
midst of this absence? Where do you go? What do you
try? I try all kinds of things, all my old tricks for getting
through—I try anxiety, I try bourbon. I pray, I don't pray.
I go to church; I keep going back to church. I make myself
busy, so that I don't have to look at the wall. There is
boredom here, and loneliness; there are also Eucharists
and angels. God darts by; sometimes I notice.

And then there is a third moment. It is a moment of
presence. Something has shifted, something has moved:
you are looking for God and you are looking in ways you
hadn't known to look before. Sometimes, in the days when
I felt furthest away from God, I thought that my goal was

to recover the kind of spiritual life I had once had, to get back to that glory road. Increasingly, I understand that I don't get to go back (increasingly, I don't want to). I am living in a place, a house, a room, and I begin to understand that something will show up in this room, and what shows up will be faith. I am less certain now than I was ten years ago, fifteen years ago; but I sense that this place is certain; it is sure.

Once upon a time, I thought I had arrived. Now I have arrived at a middle. If life is long, I am still at the beginning of the middle. Once I would have said, "Blessed assurance, Jesus is mine." From here, I say with the poet, "O Lord of melons, of mercy, though I am not ready, nor worthy, I am climbing toward you."

This book represents a few miles of the climb. I share it in the hope that you might find it good company for your own climbing.

preface, ii

Here is a way of telling you everything I just told you, more succinctly:

This is a book about God moving away at the same time that God took away the ground. First goes this. Then goes this. Gone are mother, marriage, the confidence of conversion. Then a small light dots the dark hills. And then two.

Still

wall PART I

The truth is simpler . . . and more alarming. [This]
is the end of religious experience, the very opposite
of mysticism. . . . We have been going round and
round the paths, and suddenly we see that our
path goes round a hole, a bottomless black pit. In
the middle of all our religious constructs . . . is an
emptiness. . . . However it is reached, the experience
is the same: the breakdown of order, the breakdown
of schemes and maps. There are no guiding lights in
the darkness; there is no straightforward religious
experience we can hold onto. If we can still pray at
all, we talk to an iron heaven, empty of signs.

—*Rowan Williams*

failure

"Who gets the face jug?"

That's my sister speaking, Leanne, the one with the enviable red hair. We are at the museum, looking at Picasso's *Segment of Pear, Wineglass, and Ace of Clubs,* and by Leanne's feet is her daughter who is not yet two. This is my niece's first visit to an art museum and she is charming everyone with her happiest ever smile and her cheeks round as biscuits. She seems charmed, too, by the art, and I find myself imagining that she will grow up to be a famous art critic and she will credit her passion and her success to this first visit to a museum, which was suggested by her aunt. Meanwhile I have no idea what the sentence my sister just uttered means.

"Come again?" I say to Leanne.

"Who gets the face jug?"

Oh. What she means is: *You and the man you were married to for five years—a man liked by everyone he meets, a man you made miserable with your own marital misery and whom you finally left—you and he recently met to divide up what people in a previous century (and lawyers still) would call movable property: the china your grandmother gave you on your wedding day, the few crystal glasses, the beds, the linens, and the pottery you so assiduously collected on all those Saturdays when you were trying to pretend everything was fine, Saturdays spent at kiln openings and craft fairs, selecting pottery goblets and teapots and candlesticks, and also a face jug* (which, by the way, he gets, and yes it is as depressing as you suspect it is that five years and promises you thought you were making in good faith come down to this).

The face jug after which Leanne inquires is one of a genre: simple ceramic vessels protruded by ugly, mismatched facial features, bulbous noses, eyes like fertilized eggs, sometimes fangs (it occurs to me that it is not unreasonable for Leanne's mind to wander from Picasso people to face jugs). In North Carolina, we like to claim that face jugs are Southern in origin, but in fact their antecedents lay in medieval Saxony, in England, in the Congo and Ghana. The one Leanne is asking after is oversized, enormous, really; it is hideous, pearl grey with higgledy-piggledy gashes of blue glaze, and I adore it; it has sat by the fireplace for three years. Face jugs are supposed to scare away evil spirits. They are supposed to bring good luck.

~

What needs to be said here about my marriage is, I think, only this: I was very unhappy for a long time, and all my explanations for that unhappiness seem pat and flat and deceptive. There are days when I tell myself *I tried everything I could* (therapy, though probably not enough of it; stick-to-it-iveness; etc.), and there are days when I think I could have tried more, tried harder, or tried something different, though I'm not sure exactly what. There are days when I see mistakes early in the threads of the marriage and I think, *If I had just paused then, and gone back and picked up the dropped stitch, then the sweater would have come out fine*, and there are days I think that even if I had ripped out and reknitted row after row, the sweater would never have been other than misshapen, unwearable.

From one vantage, the unhappiness was simple, like a simple sugar, unyielding fructose that flavored everything it touched; and from another vantage my own unhappiness is a mystery to me, and I suspect it may always be thus. The week I left, I made a lot of phone calls and

visits, telling those people I thought would want to hear
this from me directly, and not through the grapevine. One
woman said to me, calmly, not blasé, and not without generosity, "Some marriages just can't get very far," and what
I pictured when she said that was a spontaneous abortion,
and that is an image that has stayed in my mind in the
months and years since.

There are other stories I could tell you: I could tell you
about my mother sick with cancer the whole time we
were dating and dead three weeks before we married. I
could tell you about my astonishing talent for meanness
and indifference, a talent I hadn't known about before.
I could tell you about the people I gradually began to
avoid, or evade, or lie to—because I didn't want to say how
shattered things were, how confused. I could tell you what
I know, or what I think I know, about what I was trying to
do in making that particular marriage, what I was trying
to secure for myself. I could tell you everything that ran
through my head in the hours and days before I finally
moved out, to sleep in a twin bed in my priest's guest room.
I could tell you all those things, but they are beside the
point. The point is: I came to believe that I simply could
not stay married. I came to believe that I could not do this
thing I had said I would do; I could not do it; I was unable
to do it; it is a mark of my charmed life that it was the first

time I had ever tried to do something and simply failed. And it was a failure: a spectacular, grave, costly failure.

∽

Sometime during the years I was married—I do not know exactly when—God became an abstraction. God became puzzling, like field theory, and far away. My faith bristled; it brittled; it snapped, like a bone, like a pot too long in the kiln. Some days my mantra was *I will stay in this marriage because I am a Christian and Christians stay,* but other days, I thought: *if the choices are Christianity or divorce then I will just have to embrace secular humanism because I am not even sure I believe any of this anymore and it is one thing to devote twenty minutes every morning to praying when you are not sure you believe anything anymore and it is another thing to organize your whole life around a marriage you don't want to be in because a God who may or may not exist says let no man put asunder.* I was drifting out of the reach of faith, and I couldn't even say precisely why—perhaps because my sense of myself as a Christian had become so wrapped up with my sense of myself as a wife that to question one was to question the other; or perhaps because God was displeased with me, was withdrawing in displeasure. Perhaps because my religious commitments were asking too much of me (or, less nobly, asking something I didn't want to do).

And also because of the few jagged mean things good
Christian people said to me, things I shouldn't hold on
to but I do, like when a friend into whose lap I poured all
my misery said, *Well you know, Lauren, if you leave your
husband, you are leaving Jesus;* like the pastor who told
me I would be stepping out of God's favor and the pastor
who told me that however unhappy I was it would be
perforce the way of death to leave and perforce the way
of life to stay and the pastor who told me the problems
began when I didn't change my name; like the seminary
that, after we separated, canceled the class I was to teach.
Jagged words; mean; it is silly and immature of me to hold
on to them (it is only my own palms they are slicing) but
I do because the jagged things afford me the only self-
righteousness I have in this whole tedious story.

Maybe in hardening my heart to my marriage, I
hardened it to God, too.

Here: I had been a person who felt God, who felt God's
company; now I was becoming a person who wondered if I
had dreamed up God, and then a person who was tired of
her own wondering. Maybe none of it—God, Incarnation,
sin, redemption—was real and I just needed to get on with
personal growth and get back to politics, go on a peace-
keeping mission with the UN, do something other than
moon around wondering whether or not I had faith.

No surprise, then, that many Sunday mornings, I wanted to stay put on my screen porch. If God was a mere fancy, why keep showing up at Holy Comforter, hymnal in hand? I wanted to stay on the porch instead, and read the newspaper and think about the Saffron Protests in Burma. The porch is a good place to stay when you think that God is gone, made up, fictive, and when you are a person who is choosing to hold on to jagged things. You can stay there and do yoga and read Maureen Dowd.

I wanted to stay on the porch, or stay at the kitchen table, or stay in bed, but usually I didn't stay. Shortly after I moved into Ellie's guest bedroom, a friend gave me a copy of a bestselling memoir, which I'll call *Masticate, Meditate, Masturbate*. It tells the story of a woman, just recently divorced, who spends a year traveling the world, eating life-changingly delectable pizza in Naples, sitting in an ashram in India, and so forth. I read the memoir in two sittings, and then the next week, I read it again. But after leaving my husband, I didn't go to Italy. I just went, again, to church.

I went to church by habit. I went prompted by some deep-buried intuition. Most days I went brittle, like a dry cake of gingerbread. Like the hinges of an old book.

the view from ellie's house

Sleeping in this twin bed in someone else's house feels, in a word, pathetic. Who winds up here, at thirty-two, living out of a suitcase and sleeping in someone's spare room in a twin bed?

I express that very sentiment to my friend Samuel, who has known me for a long time. He looks at me and says, "Lauren, perhaps you should hold off for a moment feeling pathetic. Perhaps you should recognize that you are vulnerable and someone is showing you hospitality."

a poem at thanksgiving

Thanksgiving is our one big family get-together. Twenty-five years ago, my grandfather died shortly before Thanksgiving, and his three children committed to gathering every year thereafter. We grandchildren don't always all make it, but I try. I complain and roll my eyes about all manner of Thanksgiving impositions, but secretly I love this gathering—and there seems to be no way to reproduce it at another time of year, though we have floated the idea of, say, all taking a week or even a long weekend at the beach in June or July. The imagined summer gatherings never happen, but Thanksgiving happens.

This year, things are a little somber, a little strained. Strange, hard-to-handle illnesses have snaked through our family this year. There was a small house fire. And now it's only two weeks or so since I moved out of my house, and, truth to tell, I think everyone misses my not-yet-ex-husband, who is generous and friendly and who lent some ease and warmth to this gathering in years past. And it is three months since my grandmother died—the last time we were all together was her funeral. Our Thanksgiving dinner seems to contain a question about who we are without our matriarch: without my grandmother holding us all together, will we fall away from one another? Are we still a family at all?

We are not the kind of family to talk about these things. No one says, "What a hard fall this has been" or "Well, things are difficult, but at least we're here together." Instead, we pass the evening in small talk—there's a lot of discussion of recipes and Tony Hillerman novels, and the two BMW drivers in the family spend a long time debating the merits of different brands of tires.

Before dessert, I stand up and announce I have a poem to read. I have been rereading this poem all day. It seems to me to be the truest thing I have read in a long time, maybe ever.

"This is by W. S. Merwin," I say, and I begin:

> Listen
> with the night falling we are saying thank you
> we are stopping on the bridges to bow from the railings

we are running out of the glass rooms
with our mouths full of food to look at the sky
and say thank you
we are standing by the water thanking it
smiling by the windows looking out
in our directions

back from a series of hospitals back from a mugging
after funerals we are saying thank you
after the news of the dead
whether or not we knew them we are saying thank you

over telephones we are saying thank you
in doorways and in the backs of cars and in elevators
remembering wars and the police at the door
and the beatings on stairs we are saying thank you
in the banks we are saying thank you
in the faces of the officials and the rich
and of all who will never change
we go on saying thank you thank you

with the animals dying around us
our lost feelings we are saying thank you
with the forests falling faster than the minutes
of our lives we are saying thank you
with the words going out like cells of a brain
with the cities growing over us
we are saying thank you faster and faster

with nobody listening we are saying thank you
we are saying thank you and waving
dark though it is

I finish. This poem seems to be exactly what our family
needs this year. Things have been harrowing this year,
but still—still we say thank you, dark though it is. *What a
testimony to our God-given instinct to worship! A whole
liturgical anthropology right there in a few verses! Even
in the desolation, we cannot contain our praise; the praise
just bubbles up.* What more needs to be said, really?

For a few brief seconds, my relatives are silent (basking,
I assume, in the profundity and aptness of Merwin's
words), and then my aunt, my exceedingly astute aunt
whom I endlessly admire and with whom I almost always
agree, says, "Well, that was bleak." There ensues a brief
discussion between my aunt and one of her brothers about
whether the poem encourages lying, whether saying thank
you in the face of being robbed blind by greedy banks is
a lie, whether the poem is actually mendacious, and then
people go back to their Derby Pie.

ode on god's absence

When you find that God is absent, you do many things.
You temporize, for a while. You buy a new prayer book,
hoping that perhaps some Celtic blessings might do the
trick. Also, you buy some candles—a prayer rug—a new
CD, Gregorian chant.

You wonder if you have invented the whole thing: maybe
it is not that God has removed himself from you; maybe,
simpler, there is no God. You tell yourself you have evolved,
matured past needing a god. You narrow your eyes at your
absent God the way you would narrow your eyes at your
lover, in a fight, when he has just said something awful
and mean and true about you, the way you narrow your
eyes before you say *Fine, then!* and storm out of the room.
You are growing a carapace, to protect yourself from this

absence. You begin to turn your attention elsewhere, to any elsewhere that might pay you some attention back.

One thing you do, having stumbled into God's absence, into God's silence, is wonder at your own sin. You understand that the most straightforward explanation of this, God's absence, is that you have sinned.

(The year before I left my husband, I had a series of conversations about my marriage with a priest. The first day we met, this priest and I, I talked and talked, I told the whole story, I talked for an hour and a half, for two hours, longer. When I stopped, he said he had one question for me: he asked if I was married. I held up my left hand, still wearing its ring: of course I'm married, I said, in the voice of a teenage girl trying to explain something to her mom. He asked next about intention, what had been my intention when I vowed my vows. It took me weeks to understand what his questions meant, that he was saying something about fissure, about the splintering of the will, how very fractured my intention was on my wedding day, there in my splendid white dress. "Are you saying the marriage didn't take?" I asked. "That in a sense I never really entered the marriage at all?" *That I could just get an annulment and be done with it?* "No," said the priest, his tone tired. "I'm saying that perhaps you stood in a sacramental moment, before your priest and your community, and lied. And that is a serious sin you have to deal with.")

Time passes. You scrutinize your sin, you make confession after confession: confession in the alone company of a priest; confession in church, on Sunday morning, there in the middle of liturgy, blurry with the sound of everyone's voices, grateful for their voices and for the words of the liturgist: *The Almighty and merciful Lord grant you absolution and remission of all your sins, true repentance, amendment of life.*

Time passes. You continue to scrutinize. You remember that in years past you would walk down the street talking to Jesus, you would prattle on to Jesus like he was your roommate, while you cooked, while you ran errands, while you drove from store to store. You notice that now you talk to fictional characters instead. You read the Miss Julia novels in the tub, and then, while you drive, you talk to their eponymous protagonist, an elderly widow with a huge trust fund and no patience for fools; you pretend she's there in the front seat with you; you tell her all your problems. You talk to Deborah Knott, the judge who presides over the Margaret Maron mysteries; you would like to be Deborah Knott, or at least her cousin, her neighbor. While you are folding laundry, you tell Deborah Knott about the classes you're teaching, you ask her opinion of your shoes. You are no longer a lonely madwoman playing at being a mystic, calling out to Jesus as you walk to school. You are now like a child with imaginary friends.

"When the Word left me," Bernard of Clairvaux wrote, it was as though "you had taken the fire from under a boiling pot."

Time passes.

Another thing you think, when you have come to God's absence, is this: it is not God who is absent at all, it is you who are absent. This is a little like thinking about your own sin, but the thought has reshaped itself, maybe in a slightly more generous mold. The thought is turning more capacious, like a sweater that stretches out with age. You take a book down from the shelf. It is a favorite, a small red book by the Archbishop of Canterbury. You have given many copies of this book away. Your marginalia come from six years ago; six years ago you underlined this:

> It is not that I have a long journey to undertake in order to get to God, but that I have a long journey to my own reality. It is my heart, the centre or source of my own being, that is furthest away from my surface mind and feelings, and pilgrimage is always a travelling to where I am. . . . God is not merely, like the Prodigal Son's father, on the way to us: he is there at the heart. Or: he travels to meet himself in what is always other, eager to

recognize his own joy and beauty in the distinctness of what is not God's self. However we put it—there are countless ways—God's loving kindness is there ahead of us. Forgiveness is never a matter of persuading God of something but of discovering for myself that there is no distance to be crossed, except that longest journey to that which gives truth and reality to my very self.

You did not understand those words when you underlined them. Now, six years later, you think you are beginning to understand them.

(Something a friend said to me, long before I left my husband: *I don't know if you will get divorced. I hope you don't; I don't know if you will. I do know that, if you do, two years later you will know some things about God that you don't know now.* Later, as I was leaving, as I was packing to go to Ellie's, I took those words with me in my suitcase, with my turtlenecks and a gray wool dress and a dozen pairs of socks. I hoped my friend was right.)

At the aquarium in New Hanover County, you read that for crustaceans to mature, they regularly have to shed and regrow their carapaces. You read about crayfish, lobsters, crabs. You read that when they are molting, they are most vulnerable to attack.

Time passes.

Later, later on in God's absence, in God's silence, you think: *I cannot cajole God back.* You can try to effect your own return, but you cannot cajole God. God will return, or not, as God's own freedom dictates, as the whims of God's capricious grace direct. Should God return, you are almost sure he will seem different than however he seemed before. You begin to think that maybe you can wait in the company of God's silence and see what you can see, about this God, about yourself.

Later still: maybe this silence, this absence, is a gift. Maybe what began as punishment is being converted to gift, maybe that is how God works. Maybe this absence will become an experience of God's strangeness, God's mystery. You think: *Maybe I am being shown something here, if I would look, if I would see.* You think of these words from the prophet Zephaniah: *He will shout with joy for you, He will jump for you in jubilation, He will be silent in His love.*

Time. Passes.

healing prayer

On Sunday mornings I get up from my twin bed and go
to church and, at church, Sunday after Sunday, I join
the other sick and sad and shuffling in line for healing
prayer after the Eucharist. We gather in the far north
corner of the sanctuary; it is as discreet as it can be in a
modern church where there is just space, no walls, no
corners. Week after week I go forward, to kneel, and
cry, and to receive hands and words from whomever has
been assigned to the healing prayer station that week:
from Paul, a priest who went to college with my father,
who mentions baseball in every sermon and smells like
cigarettes and oranges, who says to me *Jesus loves you
and so do I;* from Shelly, who wears long skirts and sells

aromatherapeutic oil and knows all the healing properties of sandalwood and myrrh, who tells me to stay at the altar as long as I need to.

Some time later when my own hands are steadier I will ask Shelly to teach me how to do this. When my own hands are calmer I will discover that I want to offer other people what was offered to me. I will learn the prayers, saying, *May God the Father bless you, God the Son heal you, God the Holy Spirit companion you. May God the holy and undivided Trinity guard your body, save your soul, and in the fullness of time bring you safely to that heavenly country where we will enjoy God and one another forever.* I will pray, and I will hope that my hands are as capable of ballast and blessing as Shelly's hands, as Paul's. But that is in the future. At the moment, I just kneel here, fixed by the warmth and weight of hands, and cry.

christmas with anne sexton, dead poet

I am one of those overeducated library types who might
be expected to look down her nose at self-help books—
but the whole bookstore is a self-help section to me. When
something needs to be fixed, when I need something to
change, my first and abiding instinct is to read. I think I
can read my way to a solution. Or at least an evasion.

I have taken five books to Ellie's house: three novels, a
history of Monticello, and a book about ethics in the New
Testament. I read and reread the ethics book, specifically
the chapter about divorce, five or six times, until Ellie
suggests that perhaps I should pause, perhaps I should
read *The Economist*, perhaps endless rereading of this
chapter is not the most useful thing.

I walk past a bookstore every morning on my way to work. Most evenings, I wander in and dally. One night I buy a mystery novel set in a cookie shop; then a book on gardening, though I do not garden, but maybe every-thing would be better if I did. The next night, I purchase the complete poems of Anne Sexton. I own these poems already, but they are back at the house, and I am not.

> *I am torn in two*
> *but I will conquer myself.*
> *I will dig up the pride.*
> *I will take scissors*
> *and cut out the beggar.*
> *I will take a crowbar*
> *and pry out the broken*
> *pieces of God in me.*

She wrote her last book, *The Awful Rowing Toward God,* in two and a half weeks, in a *seizure of inspiration,* she said, just after her divorce. It was published five months after she killed herself. Her biographer says that the poems in this posthumous, suicidal book are not Sexton's finest, but to me they burn.

> *How many pieces?*

It feels like thousands.

Once, when she was in a mental hospital, a Catholic priest came to visit her. "Well," she said to him, "I've lost it all." The priest sat in her room and read her own poems aloud to her and she said, "Look, I'm not sure I believe in God, anyway," and he said, "Your typewriter is your altar." Sexton said, "I can't go to church. I can't pray." The priest said, "Your poems are your prayers." Later she said she'd like him to baptize her, and then she'd like to take Communion. He replied that she'd have to study the faith first, the councils, the creeds. "I can't do that, Father Dunn. . . . It would ruin . . . my thinking: I'd want Him to be *my* God, anyway. I don't want to be taught about Him; I want to make Him up." When he left her room, she asked him to pray for her. "No," he replied. "You pray for me."

> *God dressed up like a whore*
> *in a slime of green algae.*
> *God dressed up like an old man*
> *staggering out of His shoes.*
> *God dressed up like a child,*
> *all naked,*

even without skin,
soft as an avocado when you peel it.
And others, others, others.

But I will conquer them all
and build a whole nation of God
in me—but united,
build a new soul,
dress it with skin
and then put on my shirt
and sing an anthem.

In these last poems, she is sorting herself with religious words. She insists she has a right to be on the terrain of the sacred; she insists that religious words are the most apt words to use. I want her to take me with her when she goes to the sacred, when she says that the sacred must change shape to meet her, not just she bend and fold to fit on holy ground; when she tells the sacred that it must answer to her private experience of reality—that the only sacred on which she can stand is a sacred that makes some kind of sense in her actual life, in the real, uneasy life of Anne Harvey Sexton, not some imagined life or even longed-for life but this here real actual life, hers.

Oh angels,
keep the windows open
so that I may reach in
and steal each object,
objects that tell me the sea is not dying,
objects that tell me the dirt has a life-wish,
that the Christ who walked for me,
walked on true ground
and that this frenzy,
like bees stinging the heart all morning,
will keep the angels
with their windows open,
wide as an English bathtub.

I read those words every day during Christmas, all twelve days. Like a rosary, I say them over and over; like prayer.

movement PART II

Middles might be said to be under-theorized. There is an
abundance of work on opening and closure, but very little
discussion of . . . what comes in between. This is obviously
because the theory of the middle is taken simply to be the
theory of the work as a whole. Beginnings and endings
are marked points within the work, but the middle is just
the work itself with those points lopped off. . . . There is
however perhaps more to be said.

—*Don Fowler*

a sort of psalm, maybe

Where is God when you're lost? God is there, where am I?
This is a relationship, in some ways a relationship like any
other (except that your interlocutor is invisible, and might
be a figment of your imagination). You are talking past
each other. At best.

(Meanwhile, other people seem to be getting along with
God just fine, very well indeed. *Why not me?*)

My friend Ruth's mother once told her, "Every ten
years you have to remake everything." Reshape yourself.
Reorient yourself. Remake everything.

What struck Ruth about this was not just the insight,
but the source: she had imagined that her mother, her
steadfast, loving mother, was static, was always the same.
She didn't know that her mother had remade everything

seven times, eight times. Sometimes the reshaping is not big, not audible; not a move, a marriage, a child, a heroic change of course. Sometimes it is only here inside, how you make sense of things. Sometimes it is only about who you know yourself to be.

epiphany

> Yes, it is time to think about Christ again. I keep
> putting it off.
>
> —*Anne Sexton to Brian Sweeney, 1970*

And again, to church. Sometimes I cannot say much
about why I go to church other than what people who go
to the gym say: I always feel better once I'm there; I feel
better after; it is always good for me, not good in a take-
your-vitamins way, in a chidingly moralistic way, but in a
palpable way. Perhaps to say this is to turn religion into
therapy. But church is therapy, that is one of many things
it is, and, as my friend Mike once told me, the real problem
lies not in recognizing the therapeutic balm in the gospel;

the real problem is going through life thinking that the health you need can be found anywhere else.

In church time, it is now Epiphany. We have gathered at Holy Comforter in winter weeknight darkness for a service called the Festival of Lights; we have gathered to eat spicy Twelfth Night cake and to de-decorate the sanctuary, removing all the Christmas greenery and returning the festal candelabra to the closets in Palmer Hall. All year, the members of the Altar Guild have been setting aside stubs of candles too short to keep using in the altar candlesticks and the processional torches, and tonight these inches of candle fill the sanctuary, ablaze. *Surely the darkness will cover me, and the light around me turn to night,* we say. *Darkness is not dark to you; the night is as bright as the day; darkness and light to you are both alike.*

Epiphany (the word comes from the Greek for "to manifest" or "to show forth") is a season of questions and answers: who is Jesus, asks the church during these weeks after Christmas, and how can we bear Jesus' light into the world? On Sundays, we read biblical passages that "show forth" something of who Jesus is: we read about the miracles he worked, the demons he cast out, the water he turned into wine; we read about his transfiguration. This year, it seems to me that the church is posing its Epiphany questions directly to me: *You've forgotten who Jesus is?*

You've forgotten that you ever knew anything about Jesus at all? Take these weeks, and consider whether you want to remember.

The Epiphany story that most tempts my memory is the story of Jesus' baptism. There is John at the river Jordan, and there are all those unwashed people who have come for his baptism, and in the queue is Jesus, who is without sin, who shouldn't be in that line with all those sinning people: with Sam, the notorious adulterer; Jack, who's known for swindling old ladies out of their last bits of income; Lila, who's rumored to have committed infanticide; and also Mina, who's just not very nice; and Michael, the prideful prig; and Gary, who made a fortune using shady business tactics. One by one, each of these sinners appears at the head of John's line. And then Jesus appears. And John says, "I need to be baptized by you, and you come to me?" and Jesus insists.

The official reason that this is an Epiphany story is that after Jesus is baptized, a dove alights, and a voice comes from heaven declaring, "This is my beloved Son, in whom I am well pleased." The voice is taken to be the answer to Epiphany's question: this is who Jesus is—he is God's well-beloved and pleasing son. But this year, hearing in church again about Jesus' baptism, I wonder if, before the voice from heaven and the celestial dove, it is also

Jesus' standing in line by the river that tells us who he is. At Christmastime, the church called Jesus *Emmanuel,* which means God-with-us—and now he is with us in the baptismal queue. He is the One who stands with humanity in this line that is all about our sinning, our shame.

And I am in this baptismal line too, with all those tawdry first-century sinners, with the embezzler and the adulterer and the prig. I'd prefer to stand aside from them, from the woman who committed infanticide and the man who cooked the books. But I stand here too. It feels like a relief.

eucharist, i

An Episcopal church in a small town in upstate New York
has asked me to come preach. The town is home to two
vineyards, there seem to be more maple trees than people,
and the church is bedecked Gothic revival, all arches
and parapets and stone sinews you can see. I find myself
wanting to move here the minute I arrive.

At the Eucharist, I serve as a chalice bearer, following
along behind the priest, offering the cup of wine to parishioner after parishioner. Some clasp the cup and guzzle with
what looks like relish; some are daintier, more polite, as
though handling fine crystal; some don't touch the chalice
to their lips but, practicing what's called *intinction*, dip the
wafer into the wine and then consume the crimsoned host.

I don't know the people in this congregation: I don't know anything about the triplets who sport pink glasses and bobs like cloche hats; I don't know anything about the man with one arm, or the college-aged woman who surely shops at thrift stores, today clad in a polyester pantsuit circa 1969, the jacket and pants and blouse all squash-colored yellow with cinnamon trim. And it is only later, after I ask the priest, that I learn something about the elderly couple who, near the end of the Communion train, come to the rail and kneel, fragile as mushrooms.

What I learn later is that for a dozen years, he has been afflicted by a wasting disease, an intestinal disease that makes it almost impossible for him to eat—he lives on Ensure and lemonade. But at the altar I don't yet know that, I only know what I see: they each take a wafer from the priest; and when I come to them with the chalice, the wife dips as I say "The Blood of Christ keep you in ever-lasting life," and she eats her wafer, and then her husband likewise intincts his round of Christ's Body into the wine and then he hands the round of Body and Blood to his wife and she eats his wafer for him. There at the Communion rail, I don't yet know what illness lies behind this gesture, I know only the couple's hands and mouths, and that I am seeing one flesh. I have read about this, heard sermons about a man and a woman becoming one flesh; and here at the altar, I see that perhaps this is the way I come to know such intimacy myself: as part of the body of Christ, this body that numbers among its cells and sinews an octogenarian husband and wife who are Communion.

visits to my mother's grave

My forbears all lie in this cemetery, in Asheville: here, in
the half acre owned by the temple, my father's parents and
grandparents, his aunts and uncles; one day my father
will be buried here too. And there, through the hedge,
just outside the Jewish section and past a grave marker
decorated with kitchen whisks, lie my mother and her
mother. My parents had been divorced for a decade when
my mother bought these plots, but she wanted to make
it easy for my sister and me, a few steps and through the
hedge from one congregation of graves to the other. I come
here whenever I am in Asheville. I come once, sometimes
twice, whenever I am home.

When I ask him to, my father comes with me. He helps
me clear away the sodden leaves, and we place stones

on the top of my mother's grave marker, the old Jewish
custom allowing you over and over to fulfill the command-
ment of burying the dead. Once, as we walked away from
my mother's grave, my father said, "She was a complicated
woman. I was not always certain if she was telling me the
truth."

I don't think he meant about the little things: what she
had planned for the morning, or what happened at the
Junior League meeting, or how much the groceries cost.

"Maybe she was not always certain herself," I say.

⁓

I come to the cemetery and I don't know what I think
about the resurrection of the dead, or heavenly reunion.
Here I think mostly about the cold brown metal of her
grave marker; I think about how little I long for her, how
rarely I think about her; I think that she died too soon. At
her funeral someone said to me, *She died before you had a
chance to surprise one another.*

My friend Ruth once asked me what I miss about her,
and I said, "Nothing," which many days is true. And
then Ruth asked, *What would you miss if you missed
something?* She was transposing something the art critic
Peter Schjeldahl once said: when he looks at a painting he
does not like, he asks himself, *What would I like about this
if I liked it?*

What would I like about this if I liked something?

What would I miss if I missed something?

I would miss the private jokes; there was one about Gomer Pyle and Gerald Baliles, one-time governor of Virginia, and it wouldn't be funny with anyone else. I would miss the way she read to me. All during my middle-school years, she read me trashy romance novels by Susan Isaacs. Sometimes I tried to take a turn reading, but she didn't like to be read to. I would miss her obsessive interest in trees; she collected articles on native species, and when she drove me to summer camp, we would go hours out of our way to see a Quaking Aspen, or a Bigleaf Magnolia in bloom. I would miss her complexity, she was complex like a shape. I would miss the terrible way she made fun of people.

I would miss all kinds of things that didn't happen. She would have liked to know that I finally finished my dissertation and she would have liked to watch me teach a class. Those things would have given her pleasure. They would have made her proud. I wish she had gotten to retire. She would have been furious that my stepmother retired so young, and she would have enjoyed her own eventual retirement relentlessly; she would have worked at that enjoyment like a job (and she would have succeeded, as she did at every other job she ever had).

I would miss her voice. I do miss her voice; it hovers
at the edges of my amygdalae like a dream I can't quite
remember, like a poem whose meter I can recall but not
the words. I would miss asking for all the advice she died
too early to give.

I visited her grave this past Thanksgiving, the Thanksgiving of the Merwin ode, just a few weeks after I moved
into Ellie's guest room. I drove into town Thursday
afternoon and went to my father's house, and after fifteen
minutes with my happy sister and her happy husband
and their happy children, I was out the door again and
flying toward the cemetery. That afternoon, I stood by my
mother's grave and remembered the day of her burial. I
remembered: my black heels are sinking into the loam,
and here is my cousin Harriet, and my father, and the
Smiths and the Caldecotts and the McCafferys; here is
Brian, in his clerical collar and his cope; and here beside
me is the man I am to marry, and in his company, I feel
disquiet. The subtending emotion is not that I am bereft
of my mother or relieved that she is no longer trapped in a
cancerous frame, and not that I am curdled with loss; it is
just an awareness—that I should feel solaced by his steadiness, and I do not.

The memory is clear, like color. Five years after her
funeral, it is as if my mother has reached up from the grave

and pulled my head, held my head the way a person holds a cat by the scruff of the neck, and said, *There; look there.*

~~

My maternal grandmother's favorite hymn was "I Come to the Garden."

> I come to the garden alone
> While the dew is still on the roses
> And the voice I hear
> Falling on my ear
> The Son of God discloses.
>
> And He walks with me, and He talks with me,
> And He tells me I am His own;
> And the joy we share as we tarry there,
> None other has ever known.

It was written four years after my grandmother was born. I can remember her humming it in the kitchen, the linoleum floor, the green and white Pyrex mixing bowls I now wish we'd kept.

It was one of my mother's favorite hymns too, even during all those decades away from the church, and even in the last few years of her life when she began attending the Episcopal church, in whose hymnal "I Come to the Garden" is not. The day after she died, I emailed the rector of her church, and among other things I said that the hymns we would like at the memorial service were "Blessed Assurance," "Amazing Grace," and "I Come to the Garden Alone." The rector replied that these were "too Baptist: you get a C+ for hymn selection." When I wrote back, I told him these were the hymns Mom really wanted; I resisted the impulse to add that not one of them was written by a Baptist. We did not, in the end, bear Mom to the grave singing about Jesus in the garden, but the rector did give me "Amazing Grace."

The man who wrote "I Come to the Garden Alone" was a pharmacist named C. Austin Miles. He had been commissioned by a music publisher to write something that was "sympathetic in tone, breathing tenderness in every line . . . [a song] that would bring hope to the hopeless, rest for the weary, and downy pillows to dying beds." Miles sat down at the organ and opened a Bible to his favorite chapter, John 20. Ready to compose, he read again the story of Mary Magdalene's walk through the garden where Jesus had been buried, her discovery that he was alive. So the "I" of the hymn is Mary on Easter morning, but when my grandmother sang it, she became the I—the song was then about her own intimate walks and talks with Jesus, about his disclosing voice in her own ear.

During the fourth week of Epiphany, I drive to Asheville. I go to their graves and sing. It is years now after my mother's death, after her committal into this scrap of earth, but she should have the music she wanted.

I want her to know that I am trying. I am trying to pay attention. I am trying to look.

I stand here and I sing. I sing and I sing, all afternoon.

exorcism; blessing

> Whole-house, deep cleaning . . . still has a place
> for anyone who . . . likes the feeling of renewal that
> follows the major upheaval of turning your home
> inside out. . . . It is delightful to begin [a] new season
> with a home that has been scoured top to bottom.
>
> —*Cheryl Mendelson*

In the painstaking morcellation of divorce, it has been
decided that I will keep the house, so in time, I return
from Ellie's. It is a house I once loved. Now I stay at school
as long as possible. Many mornings I leave for my office
before light.

Ellie has offered to do a house blessing. I ask her,

not quite joking, for an exorcism instead; it is not my husband's spirit I wish to banish, I say, but my own, the spirit of a self who was unloving and concave. The house feels heavy, as though it is a cloth soaked in water, as though it is a very heavy bowl; it is the weight I wish to exorcise. Ellie gently but decisively suggests a blessing would be the better route.

In fact, we do neither. The weeks feel busy, and I can't quite find the energy to ritualize this move. I am not sleeping well; I don't know where to sleep. Not upstairs in the bedroom he and I once shared. Some nights I go to the upstairs guest room (which is really a nursery—it was done up for a baby boy when we bought the house, and I never bothered to steam off the cheery blue bouncing-ball wallpaper). Other nights I sleep downstairs on the couch; on those nights, I brush my teeth in the powder room and cover myself with a scratchy afghan, and I avoid going upstairs at all. Other nights I sleep on the screen porch; when the trucks from the nearby fire station howl by at 2:00 a.m., I feel I am camping out in Manhattan.

Still, no house blessing, no exorcism. Instead, one day, I call Trish, the woman who cleans Ellie's house, and she fits me in on a Monday three weeks hence for a "deep clean," the kind of cleaning you might do once a year: it involves scrubbing floorboards with toothbrushes, and taking blades off ceiling fans, and removing every book to dust. A voice in my head tells me that I should feel some measure of liberal ambivalence about paying another woman to clean my toilets and scrub my fan blades, but I ignore the voice, write a check, and leave the kitchen door unlocked. When I come home that night, it is as though my house has been visited by a whole phalanx of fairy godmothers.

A few days later, Dina is over. We are sitting in the semidark of the living room, drinking wine, not saying much. I have marveled about how terrific it feels to have a clean house, how I have slept soundly, more or less, these last three nights. Dina looks at me pityingly and says it is wonderful that my floorboards sparkle, and it is great that I have an appreciation for the ordinary wonder of a clean house (and I hear her thinking that her own house hasn't been clean since Julie and Kim were born), but it is not quite the same thing as a house blessing. "Ellie was right," Dina says. "You need more than an exorcism— Trish's deep clean is wonderful, but you shouldn't stop there."

And then Dina leaps up, and I hear rummaging in the kitchen, and more rummaging in the dining-room bookcases. She pulls down a Bible and several different prayer books, and she beckons me to the dining-room table. She has lit a candle. This table, ugly birch, was once my maternal grandmother's; it held decades of my grandmother's rum cake, her fudge cake. These days, I am mostly using the table for writing and editing, for correcting the page proofs of a book about colonial Virginia that one day maybe six people will read.

At the table, Dina makes a silence, and then she begins to read: "The greatest among you should be like the youngest, and the one who rules like the one who serves. For who is greater, the one who is at the table or the one who serves? Is it not the one who is at the table? But I am among you as one who serves." That is Jesus in the Gospel of Luke.

Next we go into the kitchen; Dina has put a few chocolate cookies out on a plate, and she has set up another candle, which she lights, and then she reads: "The cup of blessing that we bless, is it not a sharing in the blood of Christ? The bread that we break, is it not a sharing in the body of Christ?. . . So, whether you eat or drink, or whatever you do, do everything for the glory of God." Paul, to the Corinthians. We each eat a chocolate snap.

Then upstairs, to the half of the house I have generally been avoiding. In the bathroom, I wonder what Dina will read. I am unable to think off the top of my head of many pertinent texts: all that comes to mind is a snippet of Ephesians 5, possibly my least favorite chapter in the whole Bible, and decidedly not apt for the present circumstances: "Husbands, love your wives, just as Christ loved the church and gave himself up for her to make her holy, cleansing her by the washing with water through the word."

Dina lands, instead, on the prayer book's liturgy for baptism. "We thank you, Almighty God, for the gift of water," she reads. "Over it the Holy Spirit moved in the beginning of creation. Through it you led the children of Israel out of their bondage in Egypt into the land of promise. In it your Son Jesus received the baptism of John." If I were in a more punctilious mood, I might quibble about the propriety of repurposing a baptismal blessing in the bathroom. But I am not in such a mood; I am suddenly caught up in Dina's steady syllables, in the imagery of the prayer. I stop thinking about Ephesian spouses and remember instead Jesus' telling the Samaritan woman where to find living water. I think of the Hasidic rabbi petitioning God for the gift of prayer, asking *until such time as I can pour out my heart like water before You, let me at least pour out my words;* how far I am from pouring out either words or heart, but perhaps the words might begin again, and then the heart might follow.

Finally, in each of the two bedrooms, Dina reads a biblical passage about rest. And she tells me that I don't have to sleep upstairs if I don't want to.

So my house is exorcised after all, and clean, and blessed.

a thought, after reading emily dickinson

God has become illegible.

loneliness, i

I used to say to Ruth, in all those tortured months before
I left my husband, that what I feared most was loneliness.
Not being alone, which I often find perfect and peaceful,
but loneliness, which makes me want to die, which makes
me think I *will* die, which I will do anything to avoid
feeling: call a friend; go shopping; pedal endless, frantic
miles on my stationary bike; pour another drink; take
another sleeping pill.

What Ruth says is: Maybe I should try to stay in the
loneliness, just for five minutes, just for ten minutes.
Maybe the loneliness has something for me. Maybe I
should see what that something is.

Sometimes I think Ruth is a desert father reincarnated.
(Or a desert mother, of which there were a few, though we

hear about them less.) These desert people, Christians, left the cities after Christianity became the state religion of the Roman Empire. The desert people knew that the faith's new fashionableness was every bit as dangerous as the persecuting emperors of old, so they fled the cities and the temptations of ease, to find God in the rigors of the desert.

The desert dwellers didn't write much, but some of their oral teachings were eventually set down. Mostly, these desert sayings are opaque and epigrammatic; they feel like glass to me, like Jesusy zen koans. I'm sure they are profound, but usually when I read them I spend most of my time thinking that I am missing the profundity.

But there is one desert teaching that always stops me. At the center of this teaching is a young man who has gone into the desert to pursue the holy life. After a year or two of fasting, praying, and meditating on the Word, he begins to feel that his rule of life is not rigorous enough, so he goes to his teacher and asks for a more stringent discipline. The teacher replies, "Simply do this: go back to your cave, pray as you usually pray, fast as you usually fast, sleep when you are tired." The student, disappointed by this less than scrupulous response, goes to a second teacher and again asks for a more stringent rule. The second teacher says, "Go back to your cave, pray as you usually pray, eat when you are hungry, drink when you are thirsty, sleep when you are

tired." Frustrated, the young man goes to a third teacher,
who tells him, "Just go back to your cave." The point, I
think, is that you can't simply pursue God in the desert;
you must also begin to pursue yourself. You cannot fast if
you have not first noticed that you are hungry; your hunger
is what the cave can teach.

It seems to me that Ruth is saying much the same
thing when she tells me to sit with the loneliness for ten
minutes, for five, before picking up the phone, pouring the
drink, driving to the mall. Sit with the loneliness and ask
what the loneliness has for you.

loneliness, ii

I have a friend, also recently divorced, who explains to me that the loneliness he experienced in his marriage was more devastating than anything he has experienced since. "Lying in bed at night next to someone you once promised to love and knowing there is no way to bridge the gulf between you," he says. "That is the most crushing loneliness of all."

I believe him. He is describing the hideous disjuncture between expectation and reality, between what should be and what is. As Chekhov famously put it, "If you are afraid of loneliness, don't marry." Intimacy alienated—that is what my friend hates.

I happen to feel differently. I find the loneliness of no one knowing if your plane lands on time, of no one to call if you lock yourself out of your house or your alternator dies—I find that loneliness worse. The loneliness of the everyday, more than the loneliness of estrangement.

One afternoon, I try putting Ruth's advice into practice. It is a Saturday, and I am on the screen porch reading a monograph about the history of the swimming pool. It is a pale, papery day and usually this is the very thing I love most—the coolness of incipient springtime, solitude, a book. But what I want to do instead of reading this book is go strawberry picking with someone, or perhaps make a strawberry pie that I might then eat with someone; even going to the produce section of the local Harris Teeter, where I might at least see other human beings, would be better than this horrible alone reading on my porch.

The loneliness came in an instant, more sudden than weather. For the first three hours of this day, I was perfectly placid in my seclusion; now I feel as though I am about to disappear.

But I can stay in this for five minutes, I tell myself. *I don't have to exercycle or open a bottle of gin. I can ask the loneliness what she has for me.*

I tell the loneliness to pull up a seat. I notice she does not look so very threatening after all—she has a touch of the dowager about her, actually. She is clutching a handbag made of fat white beads, and she smells of rose water. We sit next to each other on my screen-porch sofa, with its faded hibiscus fabric and fraying wicker. I lean back. I breathe. I ask her where she's from, and she says over the mountain. (*What mountain*, I wonder. *I haven't lived near a mountain for years.*) I ask her what she has for me. She takes a letter opener from her bag and tells me she can kill me if she wants to.

middles

Here at what I think is the beginning of the middle of my spiritual life, I begin to notice that *middle* rarely denotes something good. Middle school—when girls turn mean, and all kids turn miserable—is that "wasteland of our primary and secondary landscape," the "crack" between grammar school and high school. And middles are often defined by what they are not: the space, the years in between that which is no longer what came before and that which is not yet what will come later. The Middle Ages are those centuries after antiquity and before modernity— and while somewhat more neutral than the baldly pejorative "Dark Ages," the term "Middle Ages" implies that the stretch of time under consideration is less interesting than the exaltations of classical grandeur or the wonders of today.

I am not thrilled by the idea that I am entering a vague in-between, after the intensity of conversion and before the calm wisdom of cronehood. I don't like to think that I am embarking on an extended sojourn into the spiritual equivalent of middle school, all insecurity and queen bee alpha girls. I begin to look for other middles, middles with more specificity, more grist.

My friend Samuel, who is a chess player, tells me about the middle game, how in chess the middle game is not merely whatever happens between the opening and the endgame. The middle game is where players stake out their strategies. There is a standard repertoire of openings in chess, only so many plausible ways to start a game—the Queen's Gambit, the Ruy Lopez. But in the middle game, very little is scripted. The middle game is where creativity begins, where tactical daring and subtlety take over. In the middle game, everything is open.

There are middles in architecture and design, too. I learn that churches of the fourteenth-century middle-point style were characterized by lots and lots of windows, whole cathedral walls given over to stained glass and tracery, trifoliate windows insistent with light.

One morning I am reading the journal of an eighteenth-century English minister. He describes hauling barley to something called a *middlestead,* which turns out to be the threshing floor of a barn, where the inedible hull of the wheat is loosened and removed. It is as if John the Baptist has called down to my library carrel, telling me the same thing about Jesus that he told his original audience two thousand years ago: "His winnowing fork is in his hand, and he will clear his threshing floor, gathering his wheat into his barn and burning up the chaff with unquench-able fire." The middle of the spiritual life may have many windows, and lots and lots of light, but it will also be a season of winnowing.

I remain on the lookout for other middles.

prayer, lively

Sometime after my mother died, after I got married, I ceased to pray. That is, I did not pray by myself, outside of churches and chapels and other places where people come together to pray. I did not pray at home, or, as I had once done, while walking. I did not drift off to sleep talking to God, as I had once done. I did not say Morning Prayer, unless I was around other people who were saying it.

I would like to say it was a daughter's bereavement choking off prayer, but I don't think that's true. I think my ceasing to pray had more to do with my marriage. I think if anything was stopping my mouth from praise or petition it was not a filial grief, but the weary, wary confusion of a wife who did not want to be married. My husband was a person of deep prayer, and prayer threatened to connect us, so I stopped. And I began to ridicule his praying; it seemed an otherworldly absurdity in the midst of all this unhappiness. I turned caustic. My energy went to keeping up appearances, and to misery. I did not save over much energy for prayer.

I told my spiritual director I was praying (I doubt she was fooled). I told myself that I should be praying, that it would be good for me to pray; I said to myself, *Of course you feel far away from God, how could you feel otherwise when you will not pray?* But still, I persisted in not praying. My chastisements about my own lack of prayer became private jokes. When I nosed up against prayer, I felt only anger. When I did not wish to feel angry, I let prayer find me numb. I could remember that some years before I had enjoyed prayer; I had actually taken joy in it. I pictured that years-ago woman and her easy, vibrant praying and sometimes I felt nostalgic and sometimes I felt superior and sometimes I did not feel any way at all.

～

Prayer, writes the poet Carrie Fountain,

> *was the last skill I learned. I practiced*
> *rigorously. Just as I was getting good, I lost it. As soon as it*
> *was gone, I understood it was not a skill at all.*

～

And then I begin to pray sometimes. I say things that
might be prayers, or might not. Or sometimes I think I
have stepped into someone else's prayer, and I stay there,
poised, ready to walk into another room; or I stay there,
heavy, like a tired hand resting on a table. Or I pick up
a pen and a piece of paper and that is a prayer, or it is
not. Or I look out the window at the fence, peeling paint,
covered in pollen, and I wonder if that is prayer.

And then, unaccountably, a shift.

The shift is a mystery.

I do not know why things shift. I've shown up for chapel
at school, and there I stand, reciting a psalm. I must
admit I have never much liked the psalms, they have never
prayed easy to me. It is, of course, absurd to offer this kind
of jejune, self-referential assessment—what does it matter
whether I *like* the Psalter or not, and how, really, can I find
the psalms (which are, after all, both time-tested poetry
and also the prayer book of the Jewish people, which is to
say among other people the prayer book of Jesus) dull, but
in fact I have found them dull for many years and mostly
an occasion for woolgathering, and then in a moment
I can only call mystery, I am standing there in chapel
reciting Psalm 25, "Turn to me and be gracious to me, for
I am lonely and afflicted," and the words still me—there at

Morning Prayer, those words are my words; they are the most straightforward expression of anything I might ever have to say to God, or to myself. For the space of eighteen syllables, I have, it seems, prayed.

I leave chapel hoping this will happen every morning now, that this is the start of my completely new and different, totally fiery relationship with the Psalter. I think I may be on my way to becoming a sort of Psalter mystic, like the first-century hermit who, after an especially heartfelt recitation of Psalm 93, was visited by the Archangel Michael, or like blessed Saint Radegund, so pious that she chanted the psalms even in her sleep.

Of course, that is not what happens. The next morning the psalms are dull again, and I am not even really paying attention; except their dullness is enlivened slightly by the small new knowledge that once (and so maybe again someday, maybe this day) the psalms prayed me. The hour is enlivened by the suspicion that maybe there is prayer even now, despite my being back to boredom.

This is a very small shift. It is just the kind of small shift that will keep me trying to pray for another two years, or three. It is a very small mystery. Most days, I continue to look at the fence, peeling, pollen.

"Without prayer," Catherine Doherty once wrote, "the life of the Christian dies." Her words scare me; I have edged closer to them than I like to admit. The problem is that your Christian life gets sick before it dies, and it is hard to keep praying when you are sick.

I can paint my walls with slogans about staying faithful to the spiritual disciplines, about formation and habits to carry you through, about how wonderful it is that we Episcopalians have this great incomparable liturgy that keeps us tethered to prayer when our own heart's a-wandering, but the simple truth is that when you don't know what you believe and you don't know where you are or you think you've been deluded or abandoned or you've glutted yourself with busyness and you are hiding from yourself or the day has just been too long—if that is who and how you are, prayer sounds like a barefoot hike from Asheville to Paris: it would be nice if you got there, you are sure there is a nice glass of wine and a nice slice of brie waiting for you at some café somewhere, but there is really no way you can imagine actually making the walk.

In those instances it can be hard even to put your body in the posture of prayer, even to open the prayer book, hard to resist the sibilant voice that tells you, lazy wretch, that you'll do it tomorrow or the tomorrow after that. Even if once upon a time you had good habits. Even if what you want is to pray.

I notice, pondering Catherine Doherty's sentence, that she does not specify whose prayer is required to keep you from dying. I notice that she says simply, *Without prayer, the life of the Christian dies.* She means, most straight-forwardly, that if you stop praying, your spiritual self will shrivel up like fruit. But her statement has overtones, and I start to suspect that the reason my Christian life hasn't completely conked out is that even when I am not praying, other people pray for me, on my behalf: Dina and Ellie and Ruth, and my dead mother from her heavenly perch, and my spiritual director, and the Blessed Virgin Mary, and some students, I'm sure, and a bishop in Virginia, and an ex-boyfriend in Maine, and possibly even the volunteer squash that has sprung up in one of the beds I haven't bothered to weed, the squash some mute testimony to bounty; I look at the squash and I think it is praying for me, I think it is prayer. All of their prayers have been in me, their prayers the blood running through my own shutting-down veins.

For which, gratitude, and the promise of reciprocation in the form of prayers from my mouth, too, or from my hands, prayers for the students and the squash, prayers

when I see an ambulance or fire truck dashing by, prayers
for people sorrowing, prayers to shield the joyous, prayers
for the farmer in the field, prayers for the woman I saw
yesterday standing in the rain, so defeated, so swamped;
she was wearing a sweater that may have once been orange
but now it was just the color of rain.

And yet again the poet: *Just as I was getting good, I lost it.
As soon as it was gone, I understood it was not a skill at all.*

pie social

We are having a pie social at Holy Comforter tonight, to
kick off our new adult-ed program. Homemade pies, a
short video; I am assigned to be a table facilitator. Around
3:00 p.m. I ask three students—students I adore, one who
is working as an intern at Holy Comforter, and two who
have recently begun worshipping there on Sundays—if
they want to go to this pie social and have a quick bite of
dinner with me beforehand. Then at 4:00 I have a really
invigorating, really fabulous phone conversation with my
spiritual director, the kind of conversation that leaves me
feeling that all is right with the world, or, at least, that
there is a way of proceeding in a world where not all is
right. At 5:00 I head to my car to go meet my students for
dinner. I am looking forward to this pie social. It is just the

kind of relaxed church event I enjoy at the end of a good afternoon.

And then I get most of the way to my car and realize that my car key—which is one of those black keypads, not really a traditional key at all—had, at some point in the day, fallen off my key chain. I look through my purse. I retrace my steps through Duke Gardens. I return to my office, look on my desk and my office floor. No key. And then, I can't draw a clear breath. This sort of quotidian, keeping-body-and-soul-together aggravation just undoes me. The fact is, I always lose my keys when things are off-kilter—one week, when my mother was in the hospital, I counted nine hours gone to looking for keys—and sometimes I wish my subconscious could be a little more subtle, perhaps inter-rupting my day with something that isn't actually such an interruption: a dream about losing my keys, maybe. Here in my office, frantic, I can't get my students on the phone, so they're waiting for me at a restaurant at which I never appear, and this role I had looked forward to—Lauren as the engaging professor who is involved in her students' lives and encourages their participation in the local parish, etc., etc.—dissolves. Finally, the intern calls me back, and in the end, she drives to school and picks me up. I tell her she should count the chauffeuring toward her ten hours of church work that week. As we walk through the doors of

Palmer Hall, the other two students hand me a plate with my missed dinner and a heavy white coffee mug filled with wine. So there I am, being taken care of by these students, instead of enacting whatever role it was I wanted to enact.

And then there is the actual adult education—the video, the discussion. Ellie tells us to take notes during the video, to jot down points we agree or disagree with; we will talk about these at our tables after the video ends. The sound (which thankfully I am not in charge of) is iffy, so half my table can't hear. As the video plays, I realize that I know several of the "talking heads"—Nora Gallagher, Phyllis Tickle, Tracey Lind; some of them I count as pretty good friends. I manage to mostly silence the crazed insecurity in my head, but occasionally it speaks up: "I have things to say about the Book of Common Prayer. I teach whole semester-long courses on the Book of Common Prayer. How come Nora was invited to be in this film and I wasn't?"

And then no one at my table will talk about what we are supposed to talk about. We are supposed to spend twenty minutes discussing our agree-or-disagree jottings. What people at my table want to discuss is the video as such— to dissect it: *it used too much insider-y lingo*, says one person; *all the featured people seemed to be well-educated*

and middle-class, says another; *not sufficiently diverse,*
all sporting expensive haircuts and dangly, craft-fair
earrings; and did you see the promotional materials? asks
a third. The promotional materials for this video series
we'll be watching together for the next twelve weeks are
apparently very low-rent—they won't do at all. I try to
channel Ellie: Ellie would know how to get these people to
talk about their reactions to the substance of the video—
their reactions to what Nora et al said about sin, Jesus, the
Holy Spirit. For the most part, I fail at that task; we say
maybe three minutes of things about Jesus, and seventeen
minutes of things about the promotional materials.

And yet: in the midst of the lost car key, the failed cool-
professor moment, the video no one could hear, the endless
conversation about posters and flyers and expensive
earrings, and my own bloated ego prattling on about
Nora the Talking Head, some part of me grasps that I am
being well fed. Some part of me—some groggy, just barely
waking-up part—sees that there is generosity here; sees
that this is the kind of potluck where you take a little sliver
of everyone's pie, because these are the gifts of the people
(well, mostly the women) of your church, and you eat too
much rather than hurt anyone's feelings, and you might
even fib a little and say the cranberry cream pie is better

than you think it is. (I think it's gross.) There is abundance
in these dozens of pies, and you eat beyond the point of
necessity and hunger, because Annie Johnson made this
and she may not be comfortable sitting around a circular
table talking about Jesus, but this is her offering, and you
will taste her pie and in that moment, God is not lost.

prayer, ii

Because it is easier to read about prayer than to pray,
I have shelves full of books: meditations on the Lord's
Prayer by a dozen different authors; scholarly accounts
of prayer in the twelfth century, the eighteenth century;
Hasidic wisdom on prayer; manuals for knitting a prayer
rug, a prayer shawl, a prayer blanket, a prayer tree. (I don't,
alas, know how to knit.) Sometimes I think that all this
reading gets in the way, that the books become excuses,
something to do in lieu of praying. Other days, I know that
to read about prayer is at least to indulge my desire, to
acknowledge that I want this thing, that I long for it, even
if this afternoon the closest I can get is reading voyeurism,
greedy spying on other people at prayer.

I read a study about children and prayer, conducted by
three psychologists in 1967. Their aim was to discover how
children's concepts of prayer evolve as children grow older.
Although ostensibly neutral social scientists, they con-
structed a hierarchy of sorts: children's ideas about prayer
don't just change—they develop; they progress from
less sophisticated to more sophisticated. For example,
children's definitions of prayer become more abstract:
the four-year-old's notion that "a prayer is about God,
rabbits . . . and deer, and Santa Claus and turkeys and
pheasants, and Jesus and Mary and Mary's little baby"
becomes, at seven, "prayer is when you ask for something
you need, like water or rain or snow," and then at twelve,
the child begins to speak theologically: prayer is how you
communicate with God, how you ask God for forgiveness.
I read the study bemused, on one page nodding along with
the hierarchy the authors are building, on another page
playfully arguing with the article, whimsically suggesting
that maybe it is not, in fact, progress when the seven-year-
old rejects the four-year-old's happy, "childish" belief that
pets can pray.

And then I come to the passage in which the authors
approvingly note that older children understand that
prayers come from within themselves. The older child
knows that "The child [is] . . . the author of his own

prayers." I realize I am supposed to think this is an advance from the younger child's idea that prayers "come from God, or from Heaven, or from Fairyland in the sky."

But I do not think it is an advance. I think it is something those children will unlearn, later, if they keep praying. I think they will come to know that the youngest children are right. I think they will come to know that their prayers do not, in fact, come from within themselves. I can participate in prayer (or not), show up to pray (or not), but I am not the author of my prayers; when they come, they come from God.

anxiety, i

I worry that avian flu is finally going to hit this year and I will get into my car and head west to my stepmother's remote farm, but I arrive too late for the quarantine, or my stepsister will pull up the same moment I do and there will only be enough food for one of us and my father and his wife will be forced into some twenty-first-century blended-family Sophie's Choice.

I worry that my identity is being stolen by someone right this second and every cent drained out of my bank account and a Lexus bought with a credit card in my name.

I worry that I have forgotten a crucially important appointment, or that I've forgotten I'm supposed to be giving a lecture in Saskatchewan and there's a small group of people sitting in an auditorium somewhere angry, wondering where I am.

I often think I've lost my driver's license. Driving to the airport, I pull out my license five times, ten times, just to make sure I wasn't somehow deluding myself when I last checked, three minutes ago back near exit 57. It's breathless, compulsive behavior, behavior that makes no sense, that has no reason. It feels like jet fuel is coursing underneath my sternum, and there is no focusing on anything other than the object of my panic: avian flu, my lost driver's license, my suddenly empty checking account.

Or I boil water for tea and as the tea is steeping I check four times to make sure I've turned the burner off, and after I leave the house I worry that the stove is on, that the house is burning down, and I call my neighbor and ask him to go check. The stove is always off.

Also I worry that I've made someone angry. A friend texts me to ask for my address and I assume she's mailing a letter to tell me that she never wants to speak to me again, and I obsess about this for seven days until I open a thank-you note for her birthday present.

One night in the fall of 2001, two men from the NYPD and two Columbia University security guards turned up at my apartment. I'd called campus security because there was a suspicious white powder outside my front door. The men at my door scooped up the powder and took it away to be tested; later they called to tell me it was not anthrax; it was Tide.

And finally, health, my own and other people's: I worry that the fleeting soreness in my father's arm is osteosarcoma; that the sudden pain in my back indicates some rare form of spinal cancer. One summer, I began feeling odd flashes of numbness in my arms and legs. Within forty-eight hours, I had forced my next-door neighbor, a pulmonologist, to admit there was a possibility that I had multiple sclerosis—*a likely possibility,* I asked, *right?* I remembered the childhood playmate whose mother had MS, I remembered her driving and then no longer able to drive, I remembered her wheelchair. When I finally got in to see a neurologist, I was told that I did not have multiple sclerosis. "The likely cause of your numbness," the doctor told me, "is stress and anxiety. You could have chosen to develop an ulcer. You chose this instead."

I suspect I come by this naturally: among my antecedents, I number the truly anxious as well as some very skilled mere worriers. My paternal grandmother was the latter, a consummate worrier. She made an art form of worrying. I think she had a roster—she could worry about only one of her offspring at a time, for about a month, and then someone else moved to the top of the list. She worried most about the big things, about marriages and health, but if there was nothing big to worry about she found something small and made it big. In one slow month when I was in college, she called to tell me that she'd been lying awake the night before, worrying about my clothes: she had taken me shopping for my birthday present, and I had chosen a long-sleeved apricot dress, and now she was concerned that I might be wearing clothes that were too old for me—clothes that were appropriate for a young married, she said, not a college student. I decided that this was sort of practice worrying, so that when the next nuptial calamity or health crisis rolled around she'd be in good shape.

My mother, by contrast, lived with anxiety. It was part of what the alcohol was about, I think, keeping the anxiety manageable. She worried about running out of money, for example. That's a natural enough fear, perhaps, for a woman who grew up sharing a bed with her divorced-and-scraping-by mother. Yet by middle age, she was a perfectly well-employed Ph.D. with a federal government Thrift Savings Plan and a long-time-ago teacher's annuity to boot.

Night after night I would see her sitting up, balancing her checkbook over and over, a dozen times in one evening, working out sums on the backs of envelopes. Eventually she inherited a small piece of land from her mother, seven flat acres in Marion, North Carolina. This seemed to still her fears a bit. She rented the land out for $2,000 a year to a man with a Dots Dario, and she told me regularly that if it came to it, she could return to Marion and put up a double-wide and make do. Even when she was dying, mere weeks before her death, she worried about tapping her savings, running out of pennies before she died; in that worry, of course, anxiety and hope twined together.

This is one of the many ways I am just like my mother. As far back as I can remember, anxiety has been my close companion, having long ago taken up residence in the small, second-floor bedroom of the house that is my body. Sometimes my anxiety takes long naps. Sometimes it throws parties. But I don't imagine it will ever tire of this neighborhood and move out for good.

～

In the ecclesial calendar, we are edging into Lent. At church, the vestments turn from green to purple. We will open each Sunday service with a litany of repentance. We will try to go with Jesus into the desert, to devote ourselves for forty days, as the prayer book puts it, to "self-examination and repentance . . . prayer, fasting, and self-denial; and . . . reading and meditating on God's holy Word." Some of us, as a token of this self-denial, will abstain from something during Lent: we won't eat sugar or chocolate, or drink any caffeine or wine. One Lent, I gave up cheese.

Left to my own devices, the most challenging Lenten offering I can come up with is salt-and-vinegar potato chips, so most years I wait to be instructed by some angel in my life, like the priest who once told me to give up reading for forty days, or the colleague who looked at me over her plastic flute of Prosecco at a Shrove Tuesday pancake party and told me that I should give up saying yes.

This year, though, we are inching toward Ash Wednesday, and no angels are turning up with my annual instructions. And so it is that two days before Lent begins, I am sitting at the island in Buck and Lydia's kitchen, complaining that I didn't know what quasi-fast to take up this season. "Maybe I should give up gummi bears," I say, popping a green one in my mouth; Lydia always keeps a small bowl of gummi bears on her island and I always bypass the bowls of healthy things like almonds and dried apricots and eat all the palest yellow, pineapple-flavored gummi bears and then all the greens.

Buck picks up his wine, in a blue pottery goblet that looks like a Communion chalice, and says, "Maybe you should give up anxiety." He is probably joking, but it seems serious to me; it seems exactly right.

"Buck," I say, "you're an angel." And I give up anxiety for Lent.

∼

One way to give up anxiety is to medicate. I tried that once, some years ago. This was in May, the first May I was married, the May after my mother died. My usual anxiety attacks seemed on the uptick, and they were alternating with periods of listless, breathless enervation. I would get up from my computer in the middle of the afternoon and lie down on the floor, unable even to walk the three yards to a sofa, and there my husband would find me when he came home from work. I hadn't moved and I hadn't slept and some days I couldn't talk to him, not even to say *Hello, welcome home, how was your day?* or *I've been here for four hours.*

This was not my first experience of these brown studies, but they had always seemed more fleeting in the past, and I had never before quite understood that when people said "depressed," they didn't mean despondent or morose; they meant actually pushed down, like what a doctor does to a patient's tongue, or what a foot does to a pedal of a pipe organ. This had been going on for some months, and friends were beginning to regale me with happy stories about SSRIs and the new wonder drug Wellbutrin. I'd always hemmed and hawed about psychopharmaceuticals,

worrying all those things that melodramatic artist-types
are inclined to worry, like that the drugs would paper over
my Real Self, that I wouldn't be able to write if I were
drugged (of course, I wasn't getting much writing done
lying there on the floor, either); but now it was May and
my new therapist—a man who would later be arrested
for allegedly filming half-clad women with a hidden spy
camera, but who at the time I thought was perfect and
wonderful and full of insight—was going out of town for a
few weeks, and I was in a panic.

The week before his vacation I told him I thought it
was time to medicate. I told him I didn't think I could get
through his trip to Avignon without drugs. He looked like
he'd been waiting weeks for me to say this, like a proud
math teacher whose pupil has finally understood how to
find the slope of a line; he said he thought what I needed
was Paxil, which would combat both the anxiety and the
listlessness on the floor, and he sent me to see the family
doctor who practiced across the street.

I loved Paxil. It made the anxiety evaporate. Also—in
combination with enough alcohol or with the sleeping pills
I had swiped from my dead mother's dresser top and doled
out sparingly to my insomniac self—the Paxil produced
lovely hallucinations, as the night when I thought that
three princesses dressed in white gowns and white pointy

hats had joined my husband and me in bed. I was quite
happy with the drug until, about six months in, I gained
twenty pounds in what seemed like two days. Wearing
this new weight, I stared at myself in the mirror for long
stretches. I borrowed a few skirts from my friend Kay. I
went to Old Navy and bought three dresses made from
a stretchy plastic-like material that I knew would fall
apart after two rounds in the washing machine. Briefly, I
tried to persuade myself that it would be good feminism
to embrace my new body. Then I returned to the doctor,
told him the twenty pounds was good for neither depres-
sion nor anxiety, and began to wean myself off the pills. I
will spare you the story of that weaning—the feeling that
my skull had been put in a juicer; the constant ringing in
my ears, each ear chiming a different note, my sense that
everything would be fine if I could just resolve the left ear's
B-flat into the right ear's B. Once the tinnitus stopped, I
started trying to lose the twenty pounds. (After four years
of sporadic South Beaching, I finally acknowledged that
half of them were here to stay.)

   That is one way to beat anxiety, and I may go there
again someday, to the pharmacists' queue—if it becomes
too unpalatable, too unmanageable. But this Lent, I will
try to give up anxiety without a prescription. "Her illness,"
Martin Luther wrote of an anxious woman he knew, "is

not for the apothecaries . . . nor is it to be treated with the salves of Hippocrates, but it requires the powerful plasters of the Scriptures and the Word of God."

∾

A text message the following week from Lydia, who wants to know how my Lenten discipline is going, and also what I will do on Easter, when everyone else I know will be eating chocolate gateau and sipping a nice glass of Pinot Noir: "Will you celebrate the Resurrection with a huge anxiety attack?"

anxiety, ii

At first, I fall back on a practice I learned well over a decade ago, when, having decided I couldn't stand one more argument with my mother about the glasses of vodka she insisted were water, I made my way to Al-Anon. That same week—apparently a week of peculiar porousness, or particular desperation—a friend made the completely shocking suggestion that my feelings needn't always get the last word in my head; that I could tell a feeling—fear, anxiety, some sort of obsession—that for the next fifteen minutes, I wasn't going to pay it any heed. After a quarter of an hour, I could go back to the feeling if I wanted to, or I could choose to ignore it for another fifteen minutes. I still live by quarter hours.

This distancing myself from a feeling for fifteen minutes

is possibly the most sanity-making practice anyone has ever offered me. It has short-circuited my spirals of hideous emotion more times than I can count, and during Lent I find myself invoking it at every turn: no anxiety for this next nine hundred seconds; maybe I will check for my driver's license or go online to see if my bank account has been hacked at 3:32, but not now.

The insight that we can exercise some control over our thoughts and feelings is deep in Christianity, at least as deep as the desert. The desert fathers spoke of the eight *logismoi:* gluttony, lust, greed, anger, dejection, listless- ness, vainglory, and pride. The *logismoi* tempt you to do destructive things—to fornicate, to overeat, to preen— and they teach you false stories about yourself: that you are dependent on food rather than on God, that you are deserving of kingdoms. The word *logismoi* doesn't translate very precisely—"passions," some people say, or "tempting thoughts." I think of the term this way: the *logismoi* are false distractions that threaten to colonize your imagination. They turn your head. They take over your brain and jerk you out of reality.

The desert saints said that the beginning of renouncing a thought is simply noticing it. That is part of what I'm doing in my quarter hours—I am noticing, and naming, and then, for a few minutes, quarantining a distraction.

But the desert fathers say something more: after noticing a thought, replace it with prayer. So that is what I try to do to my anxiety this Lent—not just ignore it for quarter-hour increments, but sidle up alongside it and pray.

～

Francis de Sales, a seventeenth-century priest and writer, addressed anxiety in his *Introduction to the Devout Life:* "Unresting anxiety is the greatest evil which can happen to the soul, sin only excepted." The anxious heart, in its flailings, loses its hold on whatever graces God has bestowed upon it, and is sapped of the strength "to resist the temptations of the Evil One, who is all the more ready to fish . . . in troubled waters." De Sales's antidote to anxiety is twofold, half positive, half negative: do pray, and do not do anything that might actually address the object of your anxiety (do not get online and check your bank balance; the action, far from steadying you, will just make you more frantic). "When you are conscious that you are growing anxious, commend yourself to God, and resolve steadfastly not to take any steps whatever to obtain the result you desire, until your disturbed state of mind is altogether quieted."

Years after I learned about quarter hours, a friend taught me a practice called saying ones. It is that simple. When the anxiety comes, start to say the word *one* over and over:

One.

One.

One.

This Lent, I say my ones slowly. It is a simple, soothing sound, and it does not escape me that *one* is a spiritual word, that one is what God is, that one is unity and wholeness; that my ones are not just a palliative litany, but some kind of truthfulness and a statement of hope, too. I have been saying ones for several years now, but I am just starting to realize they are prayers.

To help hold the ones, I learn this prayer from the back of the prayer book: "O God of peace, who hast taught us that in returning and rest we shall be saved, in quietness and in confidence shall be our strength: By the might of thy Spirit lift us, we pray thee, to thy presence, where we may be still and know that thou art God." I find myself repeating those words four or five times a day, saying them like an incantation that might drive my anxiety away. Sometimes I say the Jesus Prayer: *Lord Jesus Christ, Son of God, have mercy on me, a sinner.* In bed at night, I revert to the rhyming patterns of childhood: *Now I lay me down to sleep.* (Perhaps the refrain "and if I die before I wake" should itself produce anxiety, but it turns out to do the opposite. The prayer articulates a calming plan; the prayer describes a future. If I die before I wake, I won't find myself in a panicky, unforeseen situation; if I die before I wake, God will take my soul, and I'll be safe.)

In the middle of class one day, I am seized by the thought that I left my stove on that morning, making tea, making oatmeal, and that the house has by now long since burned down, and the fire department didn't know how to reach me, and I will come home to black hulks of char. In class we are discussing Richard Hooker's theology of the Eucharist, his claim that you can no more give an unbaptized person the Eucharist than you can feed a corpse. I think I say very little for the last half of class; it is all I can do not to bolt, run to a telephone, run home, which is what I start to do as soon as class is over: dump my notebooks on my office floor and trot out of the building and begin the two-mile walk to my house at a very fast clip, and then in the middle of the Duke Gardens I stop. I crouch down and I begin to say something from the psalms over and over: *Be pleased, O LORD, to deliver me; O LORD, make haste to help me.* These words were written by the psalmist, and then in the fourth century, the desert monk John Cassian recommended them above all other "pious formula[s]" for prayer, saying that the verse "is an impregnable wall for all who are laboring under the attacks of demons." There, crouched by the lily pond like a soccer ball, I know I look crazy, but the panic about my stove seems very real. I know I look like a desperate crazy lady talking to herself, rocking back and forth; but maybe this is just how demons attack. I am there, it seems, for a long while, repeating these words from the psalms. I mean them as I have meant very few things in my life, and I determine that I will stay by the pond for as many minutes, hours, as it takes, that I will not race home to behold my standing-up house, my not-on-fire kitchen, my half-eaten bowl of oatmeal resting calmly in the sink.

Eventually, I resume my walk home. I make myself take a turn through the art museum on my way. I make myself stop off for a grilled cheese at the diner on Ninth Street. Everything is slow. Slowly, I am beginning to see what this anxiety is about, to see its lineaments: it has something to do with being left alone to handle a situation I am not competent to handle; it has something to do with being known and unknown, with the sense that I go through life hidden, masked (all this first-person prose, even—I write it to hide in plain sight). And to the degree that I am masked I always risk being left alone—for once the mask comes off, once my friends and intimates, my charmed students, even my beloved, loving aunts see the corruptions and shames of my real heart, they will vanish, and I will be left alone with the tea-steeping house fire, left alone outside my step-mother's farm with the avian flu, alone.

Be pleased, O Lord, from this to deliver me.

manchester pilgrimage

Ruth and I are making our annual pilgrimage to
Manchester-by-the-Sea. The town is known for its architecture, for the open and modish modifications Gilded
Age architects made to familiar shingled New England
houses, the stick style house so named because of its
exposed exteriors; you can find pictures in old copies of
Century Magazine and *American Architect and Building
News*. Also Alice James, sister of the more famous Henry
and William, built a three-storied, multi-gabled, red-
brick-chimneyed "cottage" in Manchester. She entered
Boston's Adams Nervine Asylum not long after the house
was completed, and then moved to England to live near
her brother. When she wrote her will, that Massachusetts
house was the only property she owned, and she described

herself, in the will, as "Alice James, Spinster of the Town of Manchester."

Ruth and I make this trek not only for the ghost of Alice, but also for a bookstore with a deceptively twee name, Manchester-by-the-Book. Even in this age of Internet book availability, when it is harder and harder for the true bookworm to browse at a bookstall and be surprised, I am always surprised by something at Manchester-by-the-Book. On my first trip here some years ago, for example, I discovered the food writer Helen Evans Brown. At Manchester-by-the-Book I was lured in by a 1958 set of her books, three little squares with covers whose stripes and flowers recall upholstery: *Patio Cook Book; Chafing Dish Book* ("The revived and tremendous interest in the chafing dish will indubitably produce a spate of cookery books on the subject, as it did at the turn of the century"); *A Book of Appetizers* ("Like it or not, the cocktail hour has come to stay"; alas, Brown was wrong).

Today Ruth and I have come, in the pilgrim economy of writerly tourism, in search of a relic: John Updike lived for many years in neighboring Beverly Farms, and Manchester-by-the-Book received a portion of Updike's library after he died. The elaborately annotated volumes have gone to a collector with money, but scattered throughout the store are other books that once belonged to

Updike, pristine books decidedly less valuable to collectors, those he did not write in but nonetheless owned. There is, frankly, something of the vulture in me; I want some of those Updike books. I want the books he read, or even just books he kept stacked on shelves in the guest room.

The bookstore owner, on whom Ruth and I both have a small crush, kindly picks through every fiction shelf, pulling down volumes that Updike owned: Muriel Spark novellas, and Henry James paperbacks, and an Irish novelist I've never heard of, and seemingly all the novels of António Lobo Antunes; and also hardback copies of Henry Green's *Loving, Living,* and *Party Going.* Updike repeatedly said he devoted his whole life, every paragraph he put down, to learning to write like Green; I snatch those hardbacks up; they will make good talismans. There are also stacks and stacks of Updike's spare copies of his own books, heaps of *Roger's Version* and *Terrorist* and *Couples* in languages I can't identify.

After we have scavenged the fiction, we paw through Updike's religion books. I make off with three volumes of Barth; two of them I will give away next Christmas, but *Against the Stream* I will keep. Updike read Barth in his late twenties; he said the Swiss theologian helped him conquer his "existential terror." He said Barth made him "able to open to the world again," and Barth shadows

Updike's oeuvre—his novels and short stories, the interviews in which he mostly avoided religious declaration, his poems. In Updike's fictional world, many of the most compelling characters are admirers of Barth, followers of, or locked in an argument with, the *deus absconditus,* the God who hides himself. The eponymous hero of *Roger's Version,* who invokes Barth at the drop of a hat, knows that God is unknowable—knows even that God's mystery is somehow tangled up with human hope—but finds that knowledge vaguely unsatisfying. In *A Month of Sundays,* Marshfield starts out a Barthian and then becomes so far removed from God that he falls off a cliff. And Rabbit Angstrom is a Barthian, sensing that God is wholly other, that the best proof of God's existence is Rabbit's own desire for him, his own undeniable longing.

In addition to those three volumes of Barth, the bookstore's religion shelves hold one of Updike's volumes of Buber, some comparative religion texts, and several books about Hasidism, all immaculate, not a hint of marginalia; and then Ruth, who is sharper-eyed than I am, spies in Updike's copy of Alexander Schmemann's *For the Life of the World* a little something penciled on the flyleaf. (Ruth is also more generous than I; she purchases this book but later wraps it up in melon-colored tissue paper and slips it in my bag, knowing it will become my most treasured possession ever.) What Updike penciled is *Deus est qui Deum dat.* That is Augustine: God gives us many gifts, but "God is He Who gives God." This is a good thing to affirm if you live in New England, the land of the hidden God, if you say, as Updike once did, that you find attending church "generally comforting and pleasant," if you are lauded after death as a Protestant novelist by an obituary writer who thinks he's saying something quaint. I keep this book on my bedside table now, this gift from Ruth, and I open it regularly and mostly I do not read what Schmemann has to say about Eucharistic love, though I'm sure what he says is astute. Mostly I look at Updike's scribble of Augustine and I take it as a good word from a ghost, from someone entered into glory, joined up to the communion of saints; I take it as a benediction from one so keenly aware of the gulch between God and God's creatures: God is here through our longing for God; God gives us many gifts, but God is He Who gives God.

across the street
from the dickinson house

After Manchester-by-the-Sea, I drive to Amherst, where I go to the house in which Emily Dickinson lived for most of her fifty-five years. On the landing of the stairwell, a reproduction of her white dress hangs on a dummy. In the library downstairs are copies of books the Dickinsons owned—the family's Bible; the 1844 Webster's dictionary, which she said was her favorite book, her best friend.

Later, across the street in a coffee shop, I sit with the volume of Dickinson my friend Jenny gave me in sixth grade. I am hunting the poems Dickinson wrote about Jesus. She called him the "Largest Lover"—the lover willing to give his life for his beloved. The speaker of the poem tries to imitate Jesus' vast love, but finds herself too finite to love so well. In the technical language of poetry, "Largest Lover" is a *kenning:* a compressed, usually two-word metaphor. Dickinson gives us lots of kennings for Jesus. In a Christmas poem (a copy of which Dickinson reportedly sent next door to her sister-in-law and best friend, Susan Dickinson, with an iced birthday cake for Jesus), he was a "docile Gentleman" who came

> so far so cold a Day
> For little Fellowmen—
>
> The Road to Bethlehem
> Since He and I were Boys
> Was leveled, but for that 'twould be
> A rugged billion Miles—

Elsewhere, he is the "Brave Beloved," the giver of the "Gigantic Sum," the "Compound Witness" ("compound" because his life does two things—it testifies to God's love, and it transforms death), the "man that knew the News," and, arrestingly, "The Auctioneer of Parting." He is the "tender Carpenter," whose trade and compassionate temperament prompt him to nail down the lid on human suffering. He "woos" us, on God's behalf, in a "Vicarious Courtship." And he is the "Tender Pioneer":

All the other Distance
He hath traversed first—
No New Mile remaineth—
Far as Paradise—

His sure foot preceding—

The dictionary Dickinson used defined *tender* as "anxious for another's good" and a *pioneer* as "one that goes before another to remove obstruction or to prepare the way for another." This seems to me a good way to think of Jesus: sojourning before us, clearing the brush, bushwhacking, even—removing the impediments of sin, making a path that will lead us to our true selves, and to God.

Scholars debate Emily Dickinson's religiosity. She rejected the strict Calvinism of her day, they say. She wasn't conventional in her piety. I am uninterested in these debates. What I am is jealous.

You have to know Jesus well, closely, to call him the giver of the Gigantic Sum.

You must know him well to reach for him with words like Tender Pioneer.

One day maybe I will know Jesus well enough to ken.

wisdom from my friend s., which is something of a comfort

My friend S. often talks about his wife—that she feels God is there for her in a way that he does not. Unmediated. Present. *There*. When I ask if he envies her God's thereness, S. says that it's not necessarily a good thing to be so naturally receptive to God's presence. It *can* be good, he says. But then: "to be naturally anything can make one not have to undergo the training necessary to make that which is immediate a habit." His wife, S. tells me, has undergone that training, has made the immediate also habitual. But as for himself, and as for me, S. says, "one of God's gifts to some of us is just not to be immediate, so that we have to undergo the kind of discipline necessary to have what others seem to have effortlessly."

This is something of a comfort.

busyness during lent

"I thought about sloth, about how slothful I've been."

"Ridiculous. You've worked hard. I know you have, Charlie."

"There's no real contradiction. Slothful people work the hardest. . . . Some think that sloth, one of the capital sins, means ordinary laziness. . . . But sloth has to cover a great deal of despair. Sloth is really a busy condition, hyperactive. This activity drives off the wonderful rest or balance without which there can be no poetry or art or thought. . . . These slothful sinners are not able to acquiesce in their own being, as the philosophers say. They labor because rest terrifies them."

—*Saul Bellow*

Church coffee hour, after a sermon on the elliptical logic of parables: talk somehow turns to the seven deadly sins. Even in the midst of this conversation, I can't re-create how we got there, and I am a little taken aback, since usually the most meaningful thing I talk about over the doughnut holes is whether someone's grandkids are coming home for Christmas or maybe what movie you just saw. But here we are, fingers sticky with glaze, tongues turning to the deadlies. We are not even sure we can name them all. We come up with anger, pride, avarice, envy, lust, and gluttony, and then there's silence. (*Shouldn't I be able to name them all?* I ask myself. *I teach at a divinity school. I should be able to name them.*) And then, finally, Eleanor says sloth.

"Actually, I heard on NPR that people can never remember sevens," says a man whose name I don't know; he is holding a plate with at least a dozen doughnut holes. "It's something about our brains, we always leave one of the seven off." There's a pause while we each try to think of sevens. The doughnut hole man is right: I can't come up with Vassar, or the Colossus of Rhodes, or Sneezy Dwarf.

"But it's no coincidence forgetting sloth," says Geraldine. "Laziness may have been a problem for nineteen hundred years but not anymore. Busyness is the new sloth."

Geraldine's throwaway stays with me for a long time. Busyness, my BlackBerry, the feeling of never being caught up, the fantasies about myself that the busyness

fosters—this busyness is just as disorienting, just as deadly
as the traditional seven. I am deeply slothful, undisciplined
and always staring off into space or slinking away with a
novel. And yet, busyness as often as laziness supplies my
excuse: I am too busy to go to church, too busy to pray;
there's not enough time to pray, not enough time to hold
body together, let alone soul. I am too lazy to do what's
important, or hard, so I stay busy with everything else.

Two weeks later, an odd confluence of sermon and situation:

I am driving to church thinking that I don't have time
to be there. This not having time is the reason, first of all,
that I'm driving, instead of greenly embracing the fifteen-
minute walk. *Of course* everyone *is busy,* I tell myself in
the car. *Some of the people at church have children, they
must be way busier than I.* But I don't really believe it:
I think about how behind I am with grading, and about
how much work it takes to keep up a ninety-five-year-
old house. I think about the workshop I'm supposed to
lead next week in Illinois, the handouts I need to create,
not to mention the hours I'm going to have to spend on
the phone trying to figure out why the City of Durham
thinks I owe it money, and then sometime I need to go to
Raleigh to see my niece and nephew. By the time I get to
church I am worked up into what can only be called anger:

I actually am way busier than any of the other people at church (*most of them are retired!*) and frankly I think it's ridiculous that they expect me to make time to be there, at church, on a Sunday morning.

The sermon our assistant rector preaches, once I finally arrive at Holy Comforter and decide I can make time to go in, is about how each of us thinks we have too much to do. It is about how each of us feels too busy. About the pressure, our franticness, our rush. About how it is killing us, this busyness, this constant to-do.

In 1769, an Anglican priest in Virginia named William Kay preached a sermon on pride. Kay claimed this was just a generalized message—all people struggle with pride, this was a good word for the whole congregation to hear. But one gentleman of the parish, the wealthy and irascible Landon Carter, took offense. The message, he insisted, was directed at him. He demanded an apology, the parson refused, and Carter had the doors to the church hammered over with planks, Kay barred from his own pulpit.

Maybe Steve's sermon is a message to me from the Lord, I think to myself during coffee hour. *The busyness is killing us. It's killing us killing us killing us.* This seems to me very true.

Then, as I drive home: *Except that I really* am *busier than all these other people.*

Some days, even a direct word from the Lord doesn't take.

~

An acquaintance, who is teaching a course at a women's prison in Raleigh, has asked me to come speak about spiritual autobiography. Weeks ago when I agreed, it seemed like a good idea. Now the visit is upon me, and I have steamed all day with resentment: I don't have time to do this. I don't have time for the long drive in rush-hour traffic, the two hours of class—I have eleven more pressing things I should be doing tonight, I don't have time for this.

I arrive. I sign in. I am escorted to a trailer that houses a classroom and worship space. And once in the prison classroom, there is something I don't expect. It is subtle, not the kind of epiphany that would happen in a movie: not that an incarcerated woman I've never met before says something inexplicably wise and penetrating to me, as though she has special insight into my soul. No profound-if-slightly-condescending realization that at least I am not incarcerated, that my time is precious, but not in the way I usually think.

Rather, simply: I feel happy here. I am present here, more present to the actual present than I have been in a long time.

~

From deep in the tradition, from *The Cloud of Unknowing,* a fourteenth-century text from an unnamed English monk: "You only need a tiny scrap of time to move toward God."

The words slap. Busyness is not much of an excuse if it only takes a minute or two to move toward God.

But the monk's words console, too. For, of time and person, it seems that scraps are all I have to bring forward. That my ways of coming to God these days are all scraps.

purim

I don't often insinuate myself into the celebrations and
routines of Jewish life. I miss them: I miss Shabbat
dinner, I miss the rhythms of Saturday morning worship
at shul, but I feel ill at ease foisting myself upon a Jewish
community; however kind my hosts, I think I must be
unwelcome; I think my presence must be making someone
uncomfortable. Or maybe I just make myself uncomfortable. Whatever the case, some winters I gratefully accept
the invitation to a friend's Chanukah party in Chapel Hill;
I attend my family's Passover seder (the Winners' habit of
intermarriage often means there are more Christians, or
nothings, than Jews, though I am the only actual turncoat).
But that's all. Other than the Chanukah parties and the
seders, I note the Jewish calendar in my head; I sometimes

say an apposite prayer in the silence of my own kitchen; once, on Rosh Hashanah, I sat outside a synagogue in my car and read and told myself that I could hear the people praying, that I was touching their words from across the street. This year, I find that I am counting the days before Purim; I am anticipating and remembering Purim.

Purim is the holiday that commemorates the events of the Book of Esther. It is a short book, ten chapters, set in Persia near the end of the Jews' exile there. One fine day, the king, Ahasuerus, gathered together all the men of the land for a seven-day banquet, a drinking party: "wine was served in goblets of gold, each one different from the other, and the royal wine was abundant." As entertainment, the king ordered his wife Vashti to come dance naked for the men. When she refused, the king banished her for her impudence, and set about finding a new wife. He chose a woman named Esther, who he thought was beautiful; he did not know she was a Jew. Meanwhile, a member of the king's cabinet, one Haman, announced a new rule: everyone in Persia must bow when he, Haman, passed by. Most of the men and women of Persia did as told, but Esther's uncle, Mordecai, walked past Haman in the streets and refused to bow down. Haman was incensed, and he approached the king, and bent the king's ear, saying, "There is a certain people dispersed and scattered among the peoples in all the provinces of your kingdom who keep themselves separate. Their customs are different from those of all other people, and they do not obey the king's laws. . . . If it pleases the king, let a decree be issued to destroy them." The king assented—one almost gets the sense that he wasn't really paying attention. But Mordecai and Esther were paying attention, and Esther summoned all her courage and petitioned the king to stay Haman's hand. Ahasuerus did as she requested; indeed, he had Haman hanged from the very gallows Haman had built for hanging Jews.

On Purim (the word means "lots," and refers to the lots Haman cast to determine the Jews' death date), Jews gather in synagogue to read the Book of Esther aloud; the celebrations are unruly, they are like Mardi Gras; it is a day of reversal, an embodiment of the words in Esther 9: *v'nahafoch hu*, and it, Haman's decree, was reversed. People dress up in costume and wear masks; during the reading of the Book of Esther, you stomp and shout whenever the name of Haman is read—indeed, the rabbis say you are obligated to shout so fiercely that you blot out Haman's name. And people get drunk, again following rabbinical instruction: drink so much that you can't tell the name of Haman from the name of Mordecai. A midrash tells us this feasting, this carnival, is eternal: after the messiah comes, all other holidays will be rendered obsolete—no longer will Jews devote a day to fasting for repentance, or a week to remembering the Exodus from Egypt. But after Rosh Hashanah and Passover and Yom Kippur have dissolved into the peace of the world to come, still there will be Purim; still there will be the recitation of the Book of Esther, the topsy-turvy celebration, the shouting and stomping to drown out Haman's name.

I have never been a big fan of Purim. Purim is a party, it is raucous, and I always feel uneasy at a party. I prefer the more staid, bookish holidays, such as Shavuot, when, in commemoration of the revelation of the Torah at Mount Sinai, everyone stays up all night studying a sacred text. Even as a college student, I was clumsy about the revelry of Purim. Once, I got so drunk at the Purim lunch to which my boyfriend had brought me that I propositioned one of the hosts.

But this year on Purim, I don a cheap Venetian carnival mask, black plastic with magenta feathers leafing off the edges. I drive forty-five minutes to a synagogue where I think I am likely not to know anyone. I will overcome my fears about being a complicated, unwelcome guest. It is the holiday of hiddenness. I will slip into a synagogue, and hide.

The name Esther means "hidden." You may call this sacred text not the Book of Esther but the Book of Hiddenness. Esther hides her true identity from everyone but Mordecai: "*Ein Esther magedet moledetah*," says the second chapter of Megillat Esther. "Esther did not reveal her people or kindred," that is, she did not reveal that she was a Jew.

And God is hidden, too, in this book. God is not mentioned once. See this as a fulfillment of a promise made in Deuteronomy, when God says to Israel, "I will surely hide my face." Hear the hush of Esther's name in the Hebrew of that promise: I will surely hide, *hastir astir*. In Persia, the hiddenness God promised in the deuteronomic desert has finally come about.

Call it not the Book of Esther, but the Book of God's Hiddenness, the Book of God's Hidden Face. Though God is at work, God hides.

Or perhaps not. Perhaps God is not hiding, but absent. Perhaps it is not God working to save the Jews of Persia, but only Mordecai, only Esther; not God, but coincidence that a Jew wound up married to the king, in the perfect position to petition for her people. You have a choice: see God here or not; see salvation, or see only human courage; see the divine subtly at work, or see chance, luck of the draw on this day of lots.

At the synagogue I have infiltrated, a few members of the congregation stand and offer brief commentaries on the Book of Esther. One woman imagines what happened to Vashti after she was banished. Another woman teaches a Talmudic text's suggestion that Esther and Mordecai were not just niece and uncle, but were also husband and wife. A man with aviator glasses and a red beard stands and speaks of the omission of God's name from Esther's book: to comment on God's hiddenness is to tacitly comment on God's presence, he says: someone cannot be hidden, after all, if that someone isn't there. After him, the rabbi speaks: *This may be the only book where God is not named,* she says, *but God's hiddenness is in fact shot all throughout the Torah. All throughout Torah, we find people looking for God, and not finding God, because God doesn't often conform to our expectations. God is somewhere other than the place we think to look. And our sages show that you can respond to God's hiddenness in many different ways. You can, like the writer of Lamentations, respond to God's hiddenness by mourning. Or, like the writer of Ecclesiastes, instead of asking where the God you thought you were looking for had gone, ask what God is like now. Or you can respond to God's hiddenness by being like Esther: if God is hiding, then you must act on God's behalf. If you look around the world and wonder where God has gone, why God isn't intervening on behalf of just and righteous causes, your very wondering may be a nudge to work in God's stead.*

I drive home, and once there, in honor of the day, I drink too much bourbon. I have been told that Purim feasts are foretastes of the meal God will share with the righteous in the world to come. As I drink, I wonder if this is one way of naming the time in which we live: we live in a time when it is possible for God to remain hidden. I wonder: when Jesus comes back, when God consummates God's program, when redemption is complete, will it be possible for God to hide? I wonder if the trick is not drinking until you can't tell the difference between Mordecai and Haman, but until you can't tell the difference between God's hiddenness and God's presence, or perhaps until you can't tell the difference between God's hiddenness and God's absence, for that finally is the question, that is the anguish—to abide in God's hiddenness is one thing, to abide in God's absence is altogether something else.

after purim, the eucharist

Another ordinary Sunday in church: gather; kneel; confess
and be forgiven; hear the Word of God proclaimed for
the people of God; say the Creed, declaring *Light from
Light . . . through him all things were made.* Watch Ellie
hold up the bread and pronounce blessing; move forward
to the altar rail; kneel next to a woman you know will be
in chemo next week and, on the other side, next to the
mother of a dead son. As Ellie places the small round wafer
on my hungry, upturned palm, I remember something St.
Francis of Assisi wrote: for our salvation, Jesus hides in a
piece of bread.

the feast of st. joseph

In church today the Gospel reading we hear is the end
of Luke 2, that story where the boy Jesus stays back in
Jerusalem at the Temple and his parents don't know where
he is and it takes them three days to find him. After church
my friend Samuel says to me, "Of all the Gospel readings,
that was the one that most got me as a kid! How on earth
do parents *lose* a child?"

There are all kinds of loss that "losing Jesus" might
name: perhaps a change in religious experience; you sense
Jesus' presence, intimately, and then you don't. Or you
lose Jesus because you have departed from Jesus' norm,
from his path: you begin to take for granted that he is next
to you; you head home after some intense temple experience and just assume that the direction in which you're

walking is the direction in which he's walking, and your assumption, it turns out, is wrong. Then perhaps there is a third kind of loss—the loss that comes when you notice the limits of your knowledge of God, when you feel bereft of guidance, when you feel the loss of God's saving power or of God's grace. This feeling of loss is really a way of noting, and mourning, God's hiddenness. This is the loss you name when you ask why God does not answer your prayers. It is the loss entailed when you realize that Jesus is more mysterious and more inscrutable than you had at first understood.

I tell Samuel that I have great sympathy for Mary and Joseph. I lose Jesus all the time.

A week later, I drive to D.C. During the daytime, I read an eighteenth-century diary in the Library of Congress. At night, I visit a friend who grew up in a warm church home, who worked as a youth minister for two years after college before going back to school; she is now a pastry chef. Sometime in the last year, my friend began to realize that she had lost Jesus. She says he seems to have withdrawn from her utterly. I am sitting in her living room, grading papers about fasting, as my friend rests on the couch. I think she is asleep, but later she tells me she had been praying: *God,* she said, *I don't know who you are or what you are like, but I miss you.*

When she tells me this, I say nothing—which I think is better than saying something stupid and ham-fisted, better than saying, "Oh, you're having a dry spell. We've all had them," better than cavalierly invoking the dark night of the soul. Silent better than peremptory. Silent, the better to receive what she has said.

The following Wednesday, I am at the small midweek healing Eucharist at St. Luke's. This is a service attended mostly by elderly people, people with walkers, with shakes. They come for Ellie's hands, for the oil, for the hope that Jesus will "drive away all sickness of body and spirit," and give peace. Perhaps also they come because it is something to do in the middle of an endless Wednesday. Today, a small woman named Sue, not old but with her own need of healing, leads us in the prayers of the people. She bids us pray "for all who seek God, or a deeper knowledge of God," saying, "Pray that they may find and be found by God." I pray this for my friend in Washington, and for myself.

another good reason
to go to church

In the Sunday *Washington Post* is an article by a woman whose marriage had imploded, and who had just had a massive fight with her best friend. She doesn't hold much truck with organized religion, but nonetheless, she says, "I was in dire need of people who would be nice to me for less than $125 an hour. So off I went to church."

boredom

When my friend Molly's boys were in grammar school, she instituted a new household rule: no one was allowed to say the word *bored*. It was as forbidden as a curse word. It is a good rule, one I have considered adopting for myself.

The realization that I was bored with all things Christian came several years ago in a conversation with Julian. We were at a wine bar in Washington, eating flatbread. Julian was talking about church, about wanting to get beyond the exhausting superficialities and abstractions we too often lapse into once we are through those red church doors. At some point in her quite eloquent comments, I said, "Yes, but don't you ever just find yourself bored with the whole thing?" I thought I was asking about Julian.

"Are *you* bored, Lauren?" Julian asked, looking up at me sharply. Her tone wasn't sharp, only her eyes. And then I understood that I was asking about myself. The whole religious life, indeed religion itself, had begun to bore me. There with my flatbread I saw that more than my sense of alienation from God in the midst of my disintegrating marriage, more than any moments of "disbelief," it was boredom that could most lastingly turn my head from the church. Or perhaps it's more accurate to say that boredom would be the means that alienation and disbelief would use to pull me away from church. A therapist once told me that boredom is the thing I dislike most, it is the state I try hardest to avoid; this was true, and I hardly needed a professional to point it out. Still, it was something of a shock to realize that I was bored with faith. In some form or fashion, religion had absorbed most of my attention for my whole adult life, even for my teenage life—it was almost all I read about, almost all I wanted to do. And now I wanted to read about Dvořák, or the history of quilts. Now I wanted to write about welfare policy. Now I wanted to go to law school.

∼

Ellie tells me, often, some variation on this theme: that I am a little too invested in how I'm feeling about church and God, and perhaps not invested enough in how I am serving church, God, neighbor. "Your life as an academic is about thinking and reflecting and analyzing," she said to me once. "A disciple, it seems to me, feels an urgency about glorifying God, but a disciple also rests in the blessed assurance that God is engaged with everything that matters, even when we aren't." It is very kind of her to call attention to my solipsism in this roundabout but persistent way.

~

Even to my own ear, my complaint of boredom sounds tinny and childish. The complaint seems to partake of the very banality boredom tries to name. Boredom sounds petulant: a demand to be entertained, to be amused.

The word *boredom* wasn't coined until the nineteenth century. "If people felt bored before the late eighteenth century," writes the literary scholar Patricia Meyer Spacks, "they didn't know it." There was ennui in previous centuries, but ennui is not boredom. In Spacks's words, "Ennui implies a judgment of the universe; boredom, a response to the immediate." I would like to dress up my own feelings with the more elegant *ennui,* or the more spiritual-sounding *acedia,* that state of spiritual listlessness and disengagement that the desert fathers described—but even the impulse to use those words is part of my effort to coat this tedium with the patina of age and angst. In fact, mine is just plain modern boredom. Boredom, to again quote Spacks, "presents itself as a trivial emotion . . . [and] can trivialize the world." One might add, it can trivialize the one who is bored, too.

Spacks is not the only scholar of boredom. Educational theorists have developed a whole literature that tries to get at what all those schoolchildren mean when they say they're bored. One hypothesis is that the students are simply naming the emotion they quite straightforwardly feel—"gifted" students given repetitive and unstimulating make-work will respond with cries of boredom. In that account, the school is largely to blame for the boredom: if only the Latin teacher would come up with something more interesting than "All Gaul is divided into three parts," students would not be bored. Another theory holds that boredom is not a self-evident state, but a strategy that alienated students use to define themselves against a task they can't or don't want to do. The second grader who doesn't understand a math worksheet he's been asked to complete, or the urban schoolchild who is asked to write a story about life on a farm, or the fatherless third grader who is told to draw a family tree might reject the whole undertaking by declaring boredom. Boredom, in this framework, is "resistance to . . . authority."

I feel a glimmer of recognition when I read these peda-
gogical studies. I remember that I started feeling bored
in church at precisely the moment that various Christian
voices were telling me to do something I felt I couldn't do,
that is, stay married. Maybe I evaded their instructions
and my discomfort by going to boredom. I couldn't quite
bring myself to say, to those Christian voices, "I reject your
authority." Like the alienated city student who doesn't
know a single thing about barnyard animals or milking, I
couldn't get the words out—"I don't know how to do what
you're telling me to do." So I distanced myself from the
whole thing: *I'm bored.*

~

Everywhere around me, parents are signing their kids
up for summer camp. Dina's elder daughter is going to
arboretum camp for one week, arts camp the next. "There
are so many amazing options," Dina marvels. "It makes
me wish I were eight years old again myself." One friend,
Hannah, is largely keeping her kids out of camp, signing
them up for two weeks at the Y, but otherwise giving them
lots of fallow time. "Won't they get bored?" I ask. "Oh," says
Hannah, "I want them to be a little bored. I want them to
get a little restless. When they get restless, they have the
chance to slow down and notice something they've never

noticed before, something they wouldn't notice if they were entertained at camp all summer."

Thomas Merton, the twentieth-century Trappist monk, wrote that what we are attempting to escape when we try to flee boredom is only ourselves. Perhaps boredom is not unlike loneliness: the best response may be not to run from it, but to give yourself to it, to see it as an invitation to attend more carefully to the very thing that seems boring. One of Merton's biographers, Monica Furlong, put the matter like this: "Gradually . . . a sense of order overtakes the wretchedness of boredom, there is a movement towards stillness, and in the stillness we find God, and in God, our true identity."

Boredom is, indeed, a restless state. I am, I hope, inching toward stillness.

hospitality: an icon

My friend Sarah had a run of a few months in which—
because on principle she invites in anyone who knocks on
her door—she hung out with Jehovah's Witnesses every
Saturday morning. Each Saturday, she told them that she
wasn't going to convert, but that they were welcome to
come in for a cup of tea. They did, week after week. "I don't
think very many people let them come in," Sarah says.

Last week, Sarah opened her door to find a traveling
salesman. She invited him in, told him she was not
planning to buy a vacuum cleaner and that in fact, because
her baby was asleep upstairs, he couldn't turn on his demo
model, and then she offered him a cup of coffee. He asked
why she was offering him coffee, when she wasn't even
going to let him show her the vacuum cleaner, and she said

it was because she worships a God who has said that he may be found in any person, any near or far neighbor, any prisoner or beggar on the street, any guest. "So I'm offering you coffee because you might be Jesus," Sarah said. The vacuum cleaner salesman said it was the strangest house call he'd ever made, but he took the coffee.

in boston, theology for the middle

> I call myself a Christian by defining "a Christian"
> as "a person willing to profess the . . . Creed." I . . .
> profess it (which does not mean understand it, or
> fill its every syllable with the breath of sainthood),
> because I know of no other combination of words
> that gives such life, that so seeks the *crux*.
>
> —*John Updike*

I am in Boston, reading Lenten recipes in eighteenth-
century cookbooks, and when the library closes I find a
church for choral evensong: the service of Evening Prayer,
mostly sung. During the appointed scripture readings, my
brain flits to an article I read a few years ago, an article

written in 1960 by James Pike. Pike was an Episcopal
bishop who embraced what was at the time called the
"New Theology"—he questioned the doctrines of the
Trinity and the Incarnation, and wrote books with titles
like *If This Be Heresy*. In his later years, Pike tried to cover
up his role in his mistress's suicide, and he hired a psychic
to contact his dead son ("Have you by now heard anything
about Jesus?" Pike asked during one séance; "I haven't
heard anything personally about Jesus," James Jr. replied.
"Nobody around me seems to talk about him.") Pike died in
a wadi west of the Dead Sea in 1969.

The article to which my mind wanders during this
choral evensong, "The Three-Pronged Synthesis," was one
of Pike's most controversial. In it, Pike called for a "mytho-
logical" reinterpretation of religious teachings that had
"come out of the old verticality through the centuries." He
declared that "all the verbiage associated with the Trinity
is quite unnecessary," and he denied the Virgin Birth
(perhaps an especially pointed challenge, given that the
article was published four days before Christmas). For me
what made the article worth reading was Pike's saying that
he preferred the creed to be sung, rather than said. This
was not an aesthetic preference so much as a theological
one. There were certain claims, wrote Pike, that he could
not affirm "as literal prose sentences"; there are certain

things you "simply can't be 'prosy' about." But those things tell the truth when you sing.

At this choral evensong, I find myself thinking how wonderful Pike's formulation is—though I suspect that what I find wonderful is something other than what Pike actually meant. Pike needed to sing because the music could carry him through statements about God that he thought were false (*became incarnate from the Virgin Mary*). But there is another reason to sing. The creed doesn't just make statements about God; it also makes statements about us, about the people reciting the creed. I sing not because the claims the creed makes about God are wrong, but because the claims it makes about me may be wrong; I sing if I have arrived at a moment in the Christian life when what I think about my own faith prevents me from affirming the creed as "literal prose sentences" (and since, regardless of what I think about God, God is all those things the creed says God is, I can question my own faith without questioning the status and identity of the Triune Lord). Put more simply, Pike sang because he needed to finesse the creed's claims about Jesus; I sing because I question myself.

Frankly, James Pike was very strange. Frankly, he is not my favorite figure from Episcopal history. Frankly, I don't consider him a leading light and I wouldn't have expected to be looking to him for theological guidance. But I am learning that this is a condition of the middle: you take wisdom where you find it.

After the scripture readings, the gathered body at church stands to singingly affirm our faith:

> We believe in one God,
> the Father, the Almighty,
> maker of heaven and earth,
> of all that is, seen and unseen.
> We believe in one Lord, Jesus Christ,
> the only Son of God,
> eternally begotten of the Father,
> God from God, Light from Light,
> true God from true God,
> begotten, not made,
> of one Being with the Father.

Our chanting turns those words from unadorned declarative sentences into poems, into song, and they become true about me, again; if only for just this moment, the music folds me into the *we* of the creed. Things fracture when they get too prosy. These are words that tell the truth, when I sing.

reading the bible in eight places

Today is Holy Thursday, the day on which the church
returns to the Last Supper; we recall Jesus' instituting
Holy Communion, and trying to prepare his disciples for
what was to come. Tonight I will go to church, and we will
wash one another's feet and strip the altar, taking away all
the candlesticks and linen altar cloths, the service book,
the flower vases. We will leave the altar bare like a body
washed for burial, and we will exit the sanctuary in silence.

But it is now still morning—bright, cold—and I am at
the apogee of a cul-de-sac in a suburban office park in
Cary, North Carolina. I am standing outside an immigration detention center, one of 186 such centers run
by U.S. Immigration and Customs Enforcement. These
centers exist, in the words of Immigration and Customs

Enforcement, because "strengthening the nation's capacity
to detain and remove . . . deportable aliens is a key
component of ICE's comprehensive strategy to . . . protect
public safety."

The men and women who are brought to ICE detention
centers are typically picked up in unmarked white vans—
and indeed one such van pulls in right as we arrive. A man
is taken out of the van, led into the building; he looks at us,
he looks down, he looks like Jesus to me. A Latino friend of
mine has told me that people in his neighborhood are now
so afraid of white vans that children run away from the
ice-cream trucks that sometimes drive down the street.

So it is that on this Holy Thursday, a few of us have
gathered in this office park for a foot washing and a
demonstration. My friends and I have just barely begun
the liturgy—read a few words of scripture, and started
the actual washing of feet—when the police first tell us to
leave; those of us who do not leave could be arrested. I feel
a little sick to my stomach the whole time, but I have heard
from people more saintly than I that it is not uncommon to
feel queasy when you are on sacred ground. Finally, after
three or four hours, an immigration official announces that
they have decided not to arrest us; we can stay as long as
we want. This is a good strategy; shortly after the threat
of arrest evaporates, we all go home. But before we leave,

we have a moment of prayer, and one among us, Patrick, opens a devotional to do a reading, and to my surprise, the reading is not from Isaiah or Ezekiel. It is not—overtly— about liberating the captives or returning exiled people to their homes. It is 1 Corinthians 13, a passage I usually hear at weddings or encounter on a bookmark or a piece of cross-stitch, names of bride and groom winding around the border.

Love is patient; love is kind. . . . It bears all things, believes all things, hopes all things, endures all things. Love never ends. Typically, when this passage is read, my ears glaze over; it could be a Hallmark card. But at the ICE center in Cary, St. Paul's words to the Corinthians confound. I try to listen to Patrick, but I am struggling to place this hackneyed hymn to love in the office park, in the detention center, where the central white object is not a faux-virginal dress, sweet like a pavlova, but a van for rounding people up.

And then, in the confusing space of the detention-center parking lot, I begin to hear the words. I begin to hear that what Paul meant was nothing to do with Valentine's Day; that when Paul said Love, he was not speaking about a feeling or even a way of treating the people close to you; that when Paul said Love, he was speaking about the identity of another man who was once arrested on Holy Thursday.

~⌐

Later, I learned from a colleague that what we had been
doing with the Bible at that detention center had a name:
"dislocated exegesis," that is, the practice of reading
scripture in unexpected places, in places that might
unsettle the assumptions you were likely to bring to the
text. My colleague is in the habit of taking a Bible and
a group of students to a bank and there reading Jesus'
words about money—those words usually sound different
at the bank than they do safe inside some well-appointed
suburban church sanctuary. This dislocated exegesis makes
a kind of intuitive sense to me: where you read changes
how you read; the blush-colored walls of my cunning
Craftsman house might keep some readings out. And so
I begin an experiment: once a week, in some place where
I find myself, some place other than home, I carve out a
half hour or so and read some scripture. Like every other
spiritual practice with which I have any acquaintance, it
doesn't always work, if working means producing startling
insights or some sort of spiritual uplift. Sometimes I don't
get much further than an elementary question like *what
can this promise of healing mean here in the Duke oncology
unit?* Sometimes, I get a little further.

On one occasion, I am outside an insurance building
in Hartford, the insurance capital of the world, reading

Jesus' injunctions in Matthew: "Do not worry about your life, what you will eat or drink; or about your body, what you will wear. . . . Look at the birds of the air; they do not sow or reap or store away in barns, and yet your heavenly Father feeds them. Are you not much more valuable than they? . . . So do not worry, saying, 'What shall we eat?' or 'What shall we drink?' or 'What shall we wear?' For . . . your heavenly Father knows that you need [these things]."

On a second occasion I am on an airplane reading God's description of lifting up the children of Israel on eagles' wings.

On a third occasion I am at a friend's wedding. It turns out there is something worse than attending a wedding where you don't know anyone: attending a wedding where you know six people, and they are all your ex-husband's best friends. Slipping away from the hors-d'oeuvres-and-punch table, I find myself at the end of Revelation, "And he saith unto me, Write, Blessed are they which are called unto the marriage supper of the Lamb." I have a feeling I am going to see these same six there, too.

Or after listening to a presentation at church about how our pollution makes its way through the Eno River all the way to the Pamlico Sound, I sit by the Eno and read about the leper Naaman, who immersed himself seven times in the river Jordan; his skin "became clean like that of a young boy."

Or I am outside the Bank of America Corporate Center in Charlotte, the tallest building in the state, reading about the tower of Babel.

Or I am at my father's house, and the Shabbat candlesticks are right behind me, and I read the resurrection scene in John: the disciples are in the upper room, with the doors locked "for fear of the Jews."

~

It is altogether odd that I am doing this. Although for most of my sentient life I have lived in religious communities in which people are encouraged to read the Bible, I never have actually read it much myself. Despite my rants about culturally illiterate students who know too little scripture to pick up literary allusions in *Moby Dick* or Dante, despite my official profession that the Bible is holy writ, divine revelation, a place where God speaks, I have often shrugged off the Bible as tedious and alien. Instead of reading the Bible, I have read mystics, or novels by Barbara Pym. Among some of my clergy friends this has become sort of a joke, that I actually am that Episcopalian who never knows if a given phrase I find in the prayer book originates there or was borrowed from scripture. I have envied, a little, my friends who are fluent in the pages of the Bible—not only can they quote the Bible, but they have let it inside their imagination. I have often left the Bible closed.

And now this practice of dislocated exegesis has meant, among other things, that I have started carrying a Bible around with me, which strikes me as absurd. In a novel, if you meet a Bible-toting character, you know the novelist is economically telling you that the person is either a bore, a hypocrite, or seriously pious—maybe all three. I am sure I am a hypocrite; I like to imagine I am not a bore; piety is a goal I am far from achieving.

To avoid grading papers, I begin doing some research into the image of the Bible-toting Christian. A few days into this research, I realize that, thanks to the joyous absurdities of academia, I could actually turn this into scholarship, write a paper called something like "Devout Hypocrisy: Print Media, Visual Culture, and the Bible-Carrying Christian as Cultural Artifact in Twentieth-Century Literature and Art." I could deliver this paper at a conference and get a professional brownie point or two.

My researches uncover the following:

One of the main characters in Nicholas Sparks's *A Walk to Remember* is always carrying a Bible, and this seems so important a symbol that even CliffsNotes comments on it. (Cliff concludes that it "is not a symbol of her piousness, but of her connection to the mother she never met.")

In *The Sacred Hoop*, a play based on *Black Elk Speaks*, the military commander who gives orders to "kill Cheyennes wherever found" carries a Bible.

Ghanaian president Kwame Nkrumah hung a giant painting in the anteroom of his office. It depicted his fighting the last vestiges of colonialism. Fleeing the apocalyptic scene are three small white men: a capitalist (so identified by his briefcase), an anthropologist (who carries a copy of *African Political Systems*), and a missionary, with a Bible.

Carrying a Bible can stand for feminist liberation, but only if, as in the modernist poet H.D.'s *Trilogy*, the pages of the Bible being carried are blank.

Dina knows I am a little uncomfortable with this marker of boring, pious hypocrisy (and now, colonialism and genocide). One day, she hands me a box wrapped in shiny blue paper. Inside is a crocodile-embossed Pepto-Bismol pink Bible cover with handles. It is tackier than whatever you're picturing. "From the Trendsetter line," says Dina with a grin.

~

I am sitting on a bench in a museum. The museum is a five-minute walk from my office, and I come here often, to be spelled in the middle of the day by thirty minutes of silence. Seated next to me is an old white woman who is looking at a portrait of a young black man. In my lap, the Bible is open to the fifth chapter of Luke, one of Jesus' healings, this time of a man with leprosy (I confess that most of Jesus' healings blur together in my mind, like colors running in the wash). The story ends with Luke's telling us that Jesus often withdrew to lonely places to pray. *A little like escaping to the quiet of a museum,* I think. *What can it mean for a place to be lonely?*

A place, lonely like Jesus? Lonely like me?

Maybe I can make my loneliness into an invitation—to Jesus—that he might withdraw into me and pray.

holy saturday visitation

Last week, Dina called me, asked me to accompany her on
her Saturday errands. With anyone else, this might mean
grocery shopping, or the hunt for a daughter's prom dress,
or going to pick up the poster you've had framed. But I
have accompanied Dina before: her errands are visits;
visiting is her vocation, though she would say *vocation* is
too grand a term for what she does. She visits, for hours
and hours each week: members of her church who have
trouble getting out, erstwhile bridge partners of her dead
mother who are stuck in retirement homes. I have joined
her maybe half a dozen times. My suspicion is that Dina
invites me to come along whenever she sees that I have
sunk too deep into anxious self-absorption, whenever

she thinks I am morosely wallowing a little too long in whatever sorrow or drama I've deemed exigent. She doesn't lecture me, she just tries to draw me out of myself.

On this Holy Saturday, Dina has three stops to make. First we are going to visit a neighbor of hers whose daughter died six months before. "There was a crush of visitors for a few weeks," Dina says. "Enough casseroles to feed the Polish army." And then, of course, the visits stopped; friends withdrew from the tragedy and went back to their regular lives. At Peggy's house, we do not speak much of her daughter. The only mention, I think, is when Peggy says that she has been packing up some clothes to send to a cousin. I admit I tune out most of the conversation. Peggy seems as nice as she can be, but I feel like an interloper. It is not an ebullient household, but neither does it feel like a house death has just visited.

Then we drive across town to visit a woman who lives in Gracelyn Park, a very upper-crust retirement community. I've been with Dina to visit Melissa, who met Dina's mother half a century ago in their college Shakespeare class, a few times. Years before, when Melissa was checking out the local retirement communities, her pastor gave her a list of questions to ask: What hospital was the doctor on call attached to, for example? But Melissa had her own

questions: Could she bring a bottle of wine to dinner?
Did most of the other residents do likewise? And among
the unmarried residents, what was the ratio of men to
women? Melissa has outlived both her husband and her
son by twenty years. She still gets season tickets to the
local theater, and she orders a new cashmere V-neck from
Neiman Marcus every winter month: her closet is full of
wool towers in all colors, green, raspberry, peach. Melissa
is happy to see us, offers us coffee, talks about national
politics. "I am so mad at the Republicans," Melissa says,
"I could spit."

Then we go meet a friend of Dina's for lunch at the Olive
Garden. I have friends who fast the whole three days from
the Last Supper until Easter morning. I, instead, order
a baked pasta something, heavy with cream sauce and
cheese, and one of those mini-desserts, a shot glass filled
with flavorless red cake and icing. Michelle is a graduate
student in art history; she is writing about the history of
picture frames. I commiserate with her dissertation woes;
we discuss the pros and cons of EndNote and Zotero. Only
after lunch, when we are back in the car, does Dina allow
that Michelle had a miscarriage the month before, her
second in a year.

"So this is a bereaved mother tour we've been on?" I

ask. I am glad that Dina hadn't announced the morning's theme to me beforehand.

"I thought it was appropriate to the day," Dina says.

At home that night I sit before a small mosaic of the Blessed Virgin Mary, which I bought in New Mexico some years before. The Virgin has dark, dark hair and eyes the color of kale. I set a few tin candlesticks before her and put on a CD of Pergolesi, the Stabat Mater:

> At the cross her station keeping,
> Mary stood in sorrow weeping
> When her Son was crucified.
>
> While she waited in her anguish,
> Seeing Christ in torment languish,
> Bitter sorrow pierced her heart.

With the Pergolesi playing, I sit and unclench my hands and watch the candlelight. They say Mary suffered seven sorrows. Three came early, during Jesus' infancy and youth—her flight with Joseph and Jesus into Egypt, to escape Herod's murderous decree; Simeon's prophecy that one day her heart would be pierced over this son; and those panicked three days post-Passover when Jesus stayed back in Jerusalem and Mary and Joseph didn't know where he was. The other four sorrows were deferred to the end of Jesus' life: Mary's encounter with her son as he walked to Calvary; his death on the cross; his corpse being laid in her arms; and then later his body being placed in the tomb. "Is there anything about loss you haven't learnt yet?" asks the poet Nicola Slee. "If so, Mother, tell us. We are listening."

easter vigil

On the night that divides Holy Saturday from Easter
Sunday, we celebrate the Great Vigil of Easter. It is one
of my favorite liturgies of the year. We read an endless
chain of scripture, passage after passage from the Hebrew
Bible, the very lineaments of the salvation story: Creation,
the flood, the calling of Abraham. Each year we read the
passage from Ezekiel known as the Valley of Dry Bones:

> The hand of the LORD came upon me, and he brought me out
> by the spirit of the LORD and set me down in the middle of
> a valley; it was full of bones. . . . He said to me, "Prophesy to
> these bones, and say to them: O dry bones, hear the word of
> the LORD. Thus says the Lord GOD to these bones: I will cause
> breath to enter you, and you shall live. I will lay sinews on you,

and will cause flesh to come upon you, and cover you with skin, and put breath in you, and you shall live; and you shall know that I am the LORD."

So I prophesied as I had been commanded; and as I prophesied, suddenly there was a noise, a rattling, and the bones came together, bone to its bone. I looked, and there were sinews on them, and flesh had come upon them, and skin had covered them; but there was no breath in them. Then he said to me, "Prophesy to the breath, prophesy, mortal, and say to the breath: Thus says the Lord GOD: Come from the four winds, O breath, and breathe upon these slain, that they may live." I prophesied as he commanded me, and the breath came into them, and they lived, and stood on their feet, a vast multitude.

I can tell you who has read these words at our Vigil each year: Jeremy Holthouse, then the next year Pete Cintner, then the next year Lisa Kropp; I carry Ezekiel's promises in their voices around with me all year.

The Easter Vigil is one of my favorite liturgies, but tonight I am antsy. After the Old Testament readings, rather than sit through the baptisms, I slip into the kitchen to help the women who are preparing our Champagne Easter Vigil feast. I mix a gallon of punch, dust strawberries with confectioner's sugar, fold some napkins, and eventually decide to go back to the service. The baptism is ending. There will be a few more readings (Paul; Luke), an Easter Eucharist, a ringing Resurrection hymn.

So I have just received Communion, I have returned to my seat, am sitting, waiting, wondering if I should try to look like I am at prayer, and then a voice says to me, "You can stay here now." Just five words, and I know that this voice is God and what God means is that there is ground beneath my feet again, that this is the beginning of sanity and steadiness; this is the beginning of a reshaped life.

I don't typically hear voices. In fact, this is the only time I have ever heard such a voice.

I realize this is a bit of liturgical cliché, hearing this promise of revivification at the Easter Vigil.

And I realize that in five years, or ten years, or twenty years, I might not remember it so well, or trust it so much as I do right now.

And I know that a simpler explanation is that the voice came from within me, that this was myself noticing and calling attention to the ways in which I had already begun to feel stable and steady and newly alive. But that explanation, while admittedly more reasonable than my knowing the voice to be God's, is incomplete. Even on the days when I don't believe in God, I still will tell you that one night, while sitting in church, I heard God's voice, naming a resurrection of sorts, telling me I could stay.

after a lecture about
jewish-christian metaphors

A church in Raleigh has invited me to talk to their Sunday
school class about Christianity's Jewish roots. I tell them
I will be happy to give the lecture, as long as they know
that I will open by explaining why I am not wild about the
metaphor of Christianity's having Jewish roots.

After the lecture a woman comes up to me and says
she envies Jewish time, how the days start at sunset: the
Sabbath beginning Friday night, holidays always starting
the night before. "That is how my spiritual life has always
moved," she says, "like a Jewish day, from darkness and
then into light."

presence

A gray, gray day in a forest. Suddenly, between the trees—a bird as golden as a jewel. It fluttered its wings and flew away.

—*Anna Kamienska*

two conversations

I have a friend who describes himself as a lapsed atheist.

When he says this, I know I am hearing a very true thing. I tell him that, although I have never been an atheist, his words come very close, perfectly close, to explaining why I am still a Christian.

∽

Then Jesus turned to the Twelve and asked, "Are you also going to leave?"

Simon Peter replied, "Lord, to whom would we go?"

middle voice

Students are wandering, in a daze, out of a Greek class. They are stumped by the middle voice. "I just don't get it. I just don't see the need," says a girl in a purple skirt. I, too, have never been sure I understand the grammatical middle—the middle voice, which we don't have in English, but which you find in ancient Greek and also in Tamil, in Sanskrit, in Creek, in Old Norse. The middle voice darts back and forth between the active and the passive. When you are somewhere between the agent and the one acted upon. When you have something done to you. *I will have myself carried. I will have myself saved.*

Many languages that don't have a full-fledged middle voice still have what linguists call "middle markers." Begin listening closely for hints of the middle in English and you will hear *That scotch drank smoothly; politicians bribe easily.* I like these English almost-middles; their sentences wink and allure; I like to picture the sense they make. Middles imply an agent who, while not identified in the sentence, is necessary (someone is quaffing that scotch; someone is waving an envelope of cash under your senator's nose). Middles are also known by how their subject behaves. One old definition—it has fallen out of favor with some linguists, who say the many middles of the world's tongues demand more nuance, but I find it helpful nonetheless—is that the middle is used when a subject is affected by the action of the verb; when the verb somehow transforms, reshapes the subject.

Beyond that, you use the middle voice when the subject has some characteristic, some quality, that makes it partially responsible for whatever has happened in the sentence. So the middle is used in those sentences in which the subject is changed by the action of the sentence, but the subject is not just being passively acted upon; something in its own qualities, its own characteristics, is necessary for the action, too—if the scotch weren't smooth, it wouldn't drink well; if the senator weren't corrupt, she wouldn't bribe easily.

Linguists say it is hard to generalize about the many languages with middles; it is hard to categorize the many

different kinds of verbs that seem to call for the middle
voice in Old Norse, in Greek. Yet students of the middle
voice will allow that certain situations take the middle in
language after language: emotion verbs, like *grieve* and
mourn, seem to want the middle voice; so do verbs that
describe moving your body without changing your overall
position (*turn,* but not *run; bow,* but not *dive*) and verbs
that name a change in bodily posture but not much motion
(*lie down, kneel*). Also, the middle likes actions that are
necessarily mutual, necessarily reciprocal (*embrace,
greet, converse*), verbs for speech actions with emotional
overtones (*confess*), verbs of cognition (*think*), and verbs
of spontaneous happening (*grow, become, change*), as well
as verbs that capture a person caring for her own body
(*washing one's hands*).

These middle verbs, it seems to me, are religious; they
are the very actions that constitute a religious life: to
forgive, to imagine, to grow, to yearn, to lament, to meet, to
kneel. To have one's body doused in the waters of baptism.
To ponder.

All of which suggests to me that the middle is the
language of spirituality, of devotion, the language of
religious choreography. It is the middle voice that captures
the strange ways activity and passivity dance together
in the religious life; it is the voice that tells you that I

am changed when I do these things and that there is something about me that allows these happenings to happen; and yet it is the voice that insists that there is another agent at work, another agent always vivifying the action, even when unnamed.

If English had a middle voice, I would use it to speak of prayer: I would let the middle remind me that I am changed by this action, by these words, this supplicant's posture; I would let the middle tell me, too, how there is something about me that allows the action to take place—my desire, my endless need. And I would let the middle bespeak the hidden agent, the One who animates my prayer, though undisclosed, though sometimes even forgotten. If I could make English speak a middle voice, I would use it to tell you what little I know about belief, about worship, about impatience, about love. If I could make English speak middle, I would use it to say this: *I wait; I doubt; as the deer yearns for a drink of water, so I yearn. I long. I praise.*

eucharist, iii

At a church in Hillsborough, I am fed not the usual whole-
wheat Eucharistic wafers I have grown accustomed to
at Holy Comforter, but fresh-baked Eucharistic crackers
made by the children of the parish. I am told the children
bake the church's Eucharistic bread once a year, and I
notice the bread is sweet, like caramel on your ice cream;
it leaves the taste of honey on my tongue. All afternoon
I think I can taste sweetness. All afternoon, I am put in
mind of marzipan, of shoofly pie, of a sweet cantaloupe
soup I tasted years ago; I am put in mind of caramel
icing, of bees. *Taste and see that the Lord is sweet,* says
the psalmist. I realize that in this shoofly-pie Eucharistic
bread, I am being offered something about the identity
of Christ.

The psalmist wrote about God's sweetness, and so too did medieval Christians, monks, saints. Here is a twelfth-century Cistercian named Baldwin of Ford: "Jesus is sweet. . . . He is sweet in prayer, sweet in speech, sweet in reading, sweet in contemplation, sweet in compunction, and in the jubilation of the heart. He is sweet in the mouth, sweet in the heart, sweet in love; he is the love of sweetness and the sweetness of love. . . . Those who have tasted of him grow hungry, and those who are hungry will be satisfied and the sated will cry out the memory of his abundant sweetness." Translators seem to worry about all that sweetness—that the modern reader, encountering Jesus sweet in contemplation and sweet in prayer, will taste not sweet but saccharine, not sweet but syrup, cloying. For Christ's sweetness, they use other words: *dulcet; mellifluous; gracious. Pleasant,* they translate instead. *Blissful.* But the Eucharist in Hillsborough did not tell me that Jesus is pleasant; it told me that Jesus is sweet.

The Lord "was made sweet to you because he liberated you," wrote Augustine. "You had been bitter to yourself when you were occupied only with yourself. Drink the sweetness."

female saints, their intimacy with jesus

I am set afire by his ardent love coming from him and I am filled up with his presence and his sweet grace. (Margaret Ebner)

Our Savior is our true Mother in whom we are endlessly born and out of whom we shall never come. (Julian of Norwich)

O my beloved Christ. . . . I wish to be a bride for your Heart, I wish to cover you with Glory, I wish to love you . . . until I die of it! . . . Come into me as Adorer, as Restorer, as Savior. O Eternal Word, Word of my God, I want to spend my life listening to you. . . . I want to gaze on you always. (Elizabeth of the Trinity)

We are so fastened and tied as one, and the knot so knotted between us two, that no desire, or mere strength either, of any living man, will loosen or undo it. (Katherine of Alexandria)

~

There was a season when, for me, Jesus was no more and no less than the reason I had to stay in a marriage I didn't want to be in. When Jesus was nothing but Rule. I am now beginning to recollect that Jesus is Rule, but that he is also many other things: mother, bread of life, author of my salvation, the bright morning star. We are now getting reacquainted.

prayer, in the middle of saturday afternoon

God is no longer an abstraction. But God is elusive. With this elusive God, there is a certain kind of closeness, one I did not know before God became elusive, one I did not know when God was still nearby as friend. It is the closeness of invisibility, of abiding presence, of your husband in another room of the house, also reading. Close, you do not have to speak.

Chaplets—small circles of prayer beads; rosaries, but smaller—hang on the doorknobs of the bedrooms upstairs. One chaplet was given to me by a woman I barely knew, two weeks before my mother died. Another I discovered in the back of a dresser drawer. Two of the chaplets, the beads garnet and jasper and quartz, came from New Hampshire,

made by a woman who first was a nun and then became
a goat farmer and now has turned to chaplets. Upstairs,
these chaplets hang like amulets. Sometimes I hold them
without thinking a word. Other days, I count the beads as I
say the *Gloria Patri:*

> Glory be to the Father,
> and to the Son,
> and to the Holy Spirit;
> as it was in the beginning,
> is now and ever shall be,
> world without end,
> amen, amen.

I gave a chaplet from New Hampshire to my friend
Phyllis. An identical one hangs on my doorknob. On the
first Saturday of every month, Phyllis and I pray these
chaplets together; at three o'clock, every first Saturday.
We are never in the same town. For months, we do not
speak on the phone or email. We pray these chaplets for
just a few minutes, maybe as many as sixty minutes, once a
month on a Saturday afternoon.

Intimacy with the elusive God is that kind of intimacy. It
is the closeness of praying together, apart.

lecture about light

I am attending a lecture, at a divinity school in New England, about light. The lecturer is a physicist, an expert in black holes, and she is doing her level best to give a bunch of church organists and theology students and preachers some sense of the science that underpins this symbol we ceaselessly invoke: Jesus is "the light of the world"; eternity is "like a great ring of pure and endless light"; "the light of the righteous rejoiceth: but the lamp of the wicked shall be put out"; the flames of Hell emit "no light, but rather darkness visible"; and so on.

During the Q & A, someone asks how light can be both a particle and a wave. The questioner seems perplexed.

It seems to me that anyone who worships a being who is both God and man should not have so much trouble with light.

emily dickinson, may 15

Some of my most beloved saints are not really saints—no
feast days in the church, no special prayers written on their
behalf—so I improvise. I like to mark their deaths. Today is
the death of the belle of Amherst.

Emily Dickinson has compelled me since I was tapped
to play her in a school production at age nine. I wanted
to play Betsy Ross, who had more lines, actual dialogue,
and who got to sew; my entire role consisted of sitting
at a desk, leaping up from said desk, and declaiming a
sixteen-line ode to nature, "I'll tell you how the sun rose."
In the end, clad in my mother's white Lanz nightgown,
I performed my small part with a melodramatic verve
that would have made Joan Crawford seem subtle, and I
felt bereft when the play was over. I decided I liked being
Emily Dickinson, the recluse, because after all I was on

stage alone—Betsy had to share the stage with George
Washington. This experience inaugurated a thus-far
lifelong troika: a) I secretly long to try out for community
theater, but don't dare; b) I battle regularly, but probably
not regularly enough, my love of melodramatic declama-
tion, my tendency to perform rather than listen, my desire
to be the sole object of an audience's enthralled attention;
and c) I am obsessed with Emily Dickinson, with her
seclusion, with her small world of desk and window, with
what she could make words do, how she bent them; with
her beguiling consonant rhyme and eye-rhyme, a sound-
scape where *more* and *despair* are coupled; *wind* and *God*.

For the anniversary of her death, a few friends and a few
students come over. Dina brings ginger cake, made with
the recipe Dickinson herself used, all those ginger cakes
she lowered down out of her window into the waiting
hands of neighborhood children: 3 cups of flour, 1 table-
spoon of ginger, 1 cup of molasses, butter, cream, baking
soda, salt. I read a poem about forgetfulness; Sarabeth
reads a poem about a bird; Karin reads a letter Dickinson
wrote, late in life, to a judge whom she might or might not
have wanted to marry: "On subjects of which we know
nothing, or should I say *Beings* . . . we both believe, and
disbelieve a hundred times an Hour, which keeps Believing
nimble."

Here over the ginger cake it seems to me that Dickinson was describing my own state, and my own hope: the winding back and forth between belief and disbelief, the hope that such peregrinations won't drive me crazy or make me cynical but rather keep me nimble. What strikes me, too, about these words from Dickinson is that for all the hundred-times-an-hour, she doesn't seem frantic; she doesn't seem to be wringing her hands about this back-and-forth, or anxiously aspiring to a more settled belief or disbelief.

Later that night, I find myself thinking, *maybe this is a way of inhabiting faith that is, indeed, faithful; that is generative.* Maybe God has given some people belief like a pier, to stand on (and God has given those people's steadiness to the church, to me, as a reminder, as an aid), and maybe God has given others something else: maybe God has given to some this humming sense that we know nothing, this belief and disbelief a hundred times an hour, this training in nimbleness (and maybe that is a gift to the church, too).

terminology

Belief. I look it up in the dictionary and read: "Mental acceptance of a proposition, statement, or fact, as true, on the ground of authority or evidence; assent of the mind to a statement, or to the truth of a fact beyond observation, on the testimony of another, or to a fact or truth on the evidence of consciousness; the mental condition involved in this assent."

I love dictionaries. I keep an *American Heritage* on a table in my bedroom, next to a picture of my great-grandmother, and I keep an *OED* downstairs. But to find myself in this definition of belief, I have to squeeze. My mental assent to propositions; whatever the evidence of my consciousness may or may not tell me about Jesus or about the Holy Ghost—this seems to me to circle, rather broadly, around the heart of the matter.

(As Samuel once said to me, to tell someone what you believe may be to answer the wrong question—better to say, instead, what the church believes, better to use the language the church has bequeathed to us to shape our experience of journey to God—*for us and for our salvation he came down from Heaven*. Those words are the testimony of another to which the dictionary refers.)

Why I am in church on Sunday has, perhaps, less to do with belief and more to do with faith.

Here is historian Christopher Grasso writing about the religious culture of late-eighteenth-century America: "Faith . . . meant more than intellectual assent to a set of doctrines. It was a commitment of the whole self, a hope and trust that, if genuine, ought to be the foundation of an entire way of life and vision of the world."

This description makes sense to me. Or, more accurately, it makes sense *of* me.

On any given morning, I might not be able to list for you the facts I know about God. But I can tell you what I wish to commit myself to, what I want for the foundation of my life, how I want to see. When I stand with the faithful at Holy Comforter and declare that *we believe in one God . . .* I am saying, *Let this be my scaffolding. Let this be the place I work, struggle, play, rest. I commit myself to this.*

confirmation

Tonight, our church's annual rite of confirmation. In decades past, it would have been just teenagers getting confirmed, laying claim, in this sacrament, to the promises made on their behalf when they were baptized as infants. Tonight we have our share of teenagers, but they are out-numbered by adults. Some of these adults are new to any church, recently baptized; others grew up in another denomination and now wish to throw their lot in with the Episcopalians. It is a Thursday evening; everyone dresses up, brings their family or friends.

To be honest, I have always been a little fuzzy about the theological rationale for this particular service. In early-twentieth-century formulations, you became a member of the church at baptism, but you did not fully receive the gifts of the Holy Spirit until confirmation. Then, in the 1970s, the Episcopal Church revised the prayer book, and in that revision, the church boldly insisted that the full gifts of ministry and the full indwelling of the Holy Spirit came upon you at baptism. So we are left without a good explanation for what is actually happening, theologically or spiritually, at confirmation; we are left without a good explanation of why we need this rite at all. We fall back on anthropology—it's good for teenagers who were baptized as babies to have a rite of passage. Or maybe we hold on to confirmation because it helps bishops stay tied to local parishes: this is one of the few events in the life of an Episcopal parish for which a bishop is necessary; to be confirmed in the faith, you must have a bishop's hands placed on your head.

Despite my questions about what, precisely, is happening at confirmation, I have been looking forward to the service. I like to hear the bishop say, over and over, the prayer over each confirmand: "Defend, O Lord, your servant with your heavenly grace, that he may continue yours for ever, and daily increase in your Holy Spirit more and more, until he comes to your everlasting kingdom." I love hearing *more and more* repeated ten times, twenty times, like a spell. The words themselves are redundant— the prayer could simply ask that the confirmand "daily increase in your Holy Spirit" and leave it at that. But there is abundance in this repetition: *more and more, more and more, more and more.* There is endlessness in it, there is gracious superfluity. The words echo in my head all week, in the bishop's distinctive South Carolina accent, *more* with his warm wide *o* and his almost absent *r*. *More and more.*

I think of a story my friend Julian told me. She was twelve, and she was preparing to be confirmed. A few days before the confirmation service, she told her father—the pastor of the church—that she wasn't sure she could go through with it. She didn't know that she really believed everything she was supposed to believe, and she didn't know that she should proclaim in front of the church that she was ready to believe it forever. "What you promise when you are confirmed," said Julian's father, "is not that you will believe this forever. What you promise when you are confirmed is that that is the story you will wrestle with forever."

things ellie says in church

Ellie says: *The peace of the Lord be always with you.* I take this as a wish, a prediction, and a command, all at once.

Ellie reminds us who made the earth, the soil, the water we drink: *At your command all things came to be: the vast expanse of interstellar space, galaxies, suns, the planets in their courses, and this fragile earth, our island home.*

Ellie tells us to lift up our hearts: broken or sore though they might be, lift them up! And we do.

Ellie tells us that we are welcome at the Lord's table.

Ellie tells us, too, not to linger here too long. She tells us to eat this meal, and then to go back out into the world, to make the world into the Eucharist we have just received.

It is her job to tell us these things. It is her office; it is her vocation.

When I absent myself from this place—when I sleep in too many Sundays in a row; when I make myself too busy to get to the midweek Eucharist—I forget them. I come here to be reminded: *you have sinned; you are forgiven; God is present; God is risen; God is with you. You have new life.*

a sunday morning
in massachusetts

> If Christ is to visit us
> It will be on such pitiful days as these.
>
> *—Elena Shvartz*

I have been in Massachusetts all week, holed up in a retreat center trying to write an essay about mirrors—a topic that seemed wonderful, yea luminous, when I dreamed it up: the history of mirrors, the psychology of mirrors, how living in an age of mirrors, or not, shaped people's sense of themselves. But now I have actually been writing the thing, or trying to write it, and it is nothing, it is horrible, it is dust.

So now it is Sunday morning and the phone wakes me up, and my friend Peter asks, "Getting ready for the Holy Mysteries?" He asks very cheerfully. He rarely sounds any way other than cheerful.

"Well, maybe," I say. Truth to tell, I had not exactly planned to go to church. I thought I'd skip. Read a novel, perhaps, or just sit here depressed and despairing about my total inability to write about mirrors. I tell Peter how horrible everything is, how I can't put two words together coherently, how I should quit and do something different, perhaps become a librarian or a masseuse. He gently reminds me that everyone has the occasional off week, that sometimes it's not easy to write in a new place, at a new desk, perhaps I'm being too hard on myself. Then we make a plan to have dinner the following week. As we disengage, he suggests that it really might be a good idea for me to go to church, and I know he's right, so I put a cranberry-colored cardigan over my shapeless black writing dress and brush my teeth and walk out the front door; I am just half a mile from an Episcopal church. I can make the 11:00 a.m. service of Morning Prayer.

Then I make a mistake: on the walk to church, I place a phone call, to Carter. Carter and I have been friends for half my life. It is one of those sometimes more intense, sometimes less intense friendships, and it happens to be the case that Carter started calling me a bit more and emailing a bit more once it was clear my marriage was over. I'm not yet sure what exactly is happening in these more frequent phone calls and emails—I'm not yet sure what I want to be happening—but that morning I want some comfort. I want a hit of intimacy to distract me from the bad mirrors and make me feel I'm not alone in the world. This rarely works, of course, when you turn to a friend for a fix; occasionally it works, but rarely, and this morning is not one of the exceptions. On the phone, Carter is polite, but his attention is elsewhere. It's a simple thing, an unimportant thing, but it makes me feel panicky, like perhaps I am going to burst into tears.

In the narthex, the usher hands me a bulletin and smilingly asks, "And what is your name?" He's radiating kindness and helpfulness, and he's doing exactly what the How to Be a Magnetic Church ushers' guide says to do: if a woman walks into church and you've never seen her before, don't just shove a bulletin into her hand but greet her, ask her name. Church greeters are trained to greet; they are not trained to notice strangers' overwhelming desire not to speak or be spoken to.

"L-o-r-e-n?" he asks, after I tell him my name.

"No. L-a-u-r-e-n," I say. "Like Bacall."

After he identifies himself as Joe, and asks me if I'm

visiting from out of town, and then tells me he has cousins in North Carolina, and then invites me to the post-worship coffee hour, I make my way into the sanctuary. Many of the pews are empty, including, blessedly, the last pew, and I take a spot at the very end, so that I might leave the service in the middle—if my panicky feeling doesn't subside, if I start weeping, if I start to feel even more suffocated than I feel right now.

Alone in a pew: there was a time when I hated this, hated being alone in church, hated looking at all the couples and families and bouncy cherubic infants, but those feelings have left, sometime in the last few years; what once felt sorry and painful has come to feel tranquil. I am still sometimes ill at ease going alone to dinner parties, but alone in church, I feel placed. On this particular morning, the empty pew seems luxurious. The knowledge that I can slip out, quietly, any time I wish reassures; I think I've only ever done that once, left a church service before its conclusion, but on this particular morning, the possibility of leaving is what makes it possible to stay. Even the pew in front of me is empty. I feel pampered by all the space.

Then a thin woman with bright red toenails and a simple white dress slides in to my right. She is alone, too, and she looks to be about forty. She has long shiny hair and wears no ring and I decide right then that she must be recently divorced. A minute later, a man with a palsied limp and an untucked shirt and a spot of something that looks like dried mustard on his left ear takes the spot right in front of me. So much for all that luxurious space, but what did I expect: in my experience, only two kinds of people take the last pews in church—parents of babes in arms, or people who somehow feel marginal, who are unsure if they want to be in church, unsure if they *can* be in church. So actually, it is unlikely that you'll find yourself totally alone in a last pew; it is more likely that you'll find yourself with the halt, the lame, and the new mothers.

Then, as the organist is firing up the introit, a woman sidles up to my left and mumbles something, which I take to be "Is there space here?" I scrunch my legs in so that she can squeeze past me into the still-mostly-empty middle of the pew, but she doesn't move, she just keeps standing expectantly to my left, and I come to realize that she wants to sit where I'm sitting. She wants this same spot at the end of the pew. Perhaps she too is claustrophobic. Perhaps this is where she sits every week. What choice do I have? I move over. I am now sandwiched between the thin woman in the white dress and this new woman, who looks, frankly, like she has seen better days. She has a suitcase with her, and she keeps a hat and sunglasses on through the entire service, and she smells like rotten apples and like streets. She never opens a prayer book, and she never joins in a responsive reading or a hymn, but she seems to know a lot of people in the church, and she stands and sits and kneels at all the appropriate moments. She seems, oddly, entirely comfortable. But I wish she had sat elsewhere; she makes me feel trapped.

Then, in the middle of the sermon, the rotten-apple woman begins to tap her right index finger, rapidly, on her knee. It is the tapping of a crazy person, of one of the people from whom Jesus would have cast a demon. There isn't even a rhythm to this tapping, and it makes the whole pew shake. I glare at the woman, hoping she will take the hint and stop. Tap, tap, tap tap tap tap tap. Tap tap tap. Then, unaccountably (perhaps mine is actually the body possessed by a demon?) my left hand shoots out and I close my fingers over her hand, squeezing her fingers together to stop the tapping, as a mother would still a child. In an instant, I am horrified. I can't believe I have actually done what I did. My mother is surely turning over in her urn; and she is not sending me any otherworldly advice on how I might make amends.

And then, as I am blushing the color of my sweater and

thinking that it would be nice to vaporize, I realize that the woman does not seem offended, or confounded, or even surprised, and she has not shrugged off or let go of my hand. In fact, she seems to be holding my hand.

We hold hands for the rest of the service.

And that is part of what I mean when I say it is life inside this Christian story that has begun to tell me who I really am.

after the eucharist, baking

I have begun to bake again. It is a new thing, and also not
a new thing.

I first began to learn to cook in college, so that I might
contribute to the potluck Shabbat dinners I attended on
Friday nights. From my college roommates, I learned
potato kugel and cholent and sweet potato soup. I learned
one summer with a beau in Massachusetts the simple art
of stuffing a chicken with lemons and trussing it; from
another friend, how to make a starter for sourdough
bread, and how to make risotto, how to stir and stir. All
of these things I learned from friends; my mother was
once, I understand, a very fine cook; her copies of *The Joy
of Cooking* and Julia Child are well used, and people still
talk about her pumpkin pie. But in the childhood years
that I can remember, she didn't cook much; there wasn't

much room for it in the single-mother-with-a-full-time-job whirl, and how depressing to go from cooking for all those elegant married-couple dinner parties to cooking for just me, her finicky middle-schooler. We ate baked chicken breasts once a week, sometimes with almond slivers; and mashed potato pie, layered with tomatoes and mozzarella cheese; and at least once a week we ordered a pizza. By the time I was in college, she was using the oven for storage—brown paper grocery bags, a springform pan that hadn't been used since 1974.

At eighteen, nineteen, trying to learn to cook, I realized I wasn't especially gifted at this. My cooking was more memorization than intuition—following recipes I couldn't explain, miming the motions of my friends who knew kitchens the way I knew libraries. Still, I wanted be in the kitchen. The stirring, the chopping, the waiting for dough to rise; the kitchen was the one place that slowed me down.

In graduate school, in New York, I cooked less, but on many Monday nights, I would make something simple to get me through a week of studying—a pot of soup from *The Moosewood Cookbook,* a casserole, a quiche. I could always be counted on for a raspberry torte at a dinner party.

And then my mother was sick, and I moved all my worldly goods to Virginia—mostly books, but also blue enamel pots and green pottery dishes and cookie cutters shaped like cats. I rented an apartment a block from my mother's house. When the leaves were off the trees I could see her copper roof from my window. I unpacked all the dishes and the blue enamel pots, but I didn't cook much, that year in Virginia. I ate a lot of bagels. Friends invited me for dinner; I brought wine. As though it was too sad a time for cooking. As though in honor of my mother, I couldn't cook.

She died, and I married a man whose mother had taught him all kinds of culinary marvels, how to make the perfect biscuit and how to make every delicious dessert, and I let it all fall to him. He cooked almost every dinner we ate all the years we were married. In some vague way I "missed cooking": I would tell my sister laughingly how I missed it, but I was more than happy to receive—to take advantage of?—his gifts at the table. In the years we lived together, I think I cooked two things: lasagna, and a pasta dish with goat cheese and wilted spinach. I see now how lopsided this was, wretchedly so—I see how I didn't take care of him. And I see that I was overcome by, that I just couldn't get enough of, his taking care of me.

~

For a while, after I leave him, I take most of my meals at my neighborhood Italian restaurant—a margarita pizza

with (again) goat cheese and a glass of Meritage. I feel
in awe of people who seem competent in a kitchen, who
aren't intimidated by asparagus, who know how to parboil
and to braise. I notice that Ellie can whip up an Alfredo
sauce while also carrying on a conversation with me. I have
forgotten that this was once something I had known how
to do. I drive to the grocery store and once inside I panic, I
feel overwhelmed, and sometimes I leave empty-handed.

After four months of eating pizzettes at the Italian
restaurant, I decide I need to relearn the skill of feeding
myself. This seems like a good thing to do, a step in the
direction of an adult life I can imagine wanting, a life I
can imagine being satisfied to lead. I begin slowly. Not too
long after I move back into the house, my friend Suzanne
arranges for her husband to keep the kids, so she can have
a night out. Her husband thinks we are going to a bar.
Instead we go to Whole Foods, and Suzanne helps me load
a cart. "Let's not tell Mike that this is what we spent our
evening doing," she says. "He already worries that I have
too many needy and dependent friends." Later that week,
I broil a piece of salmon; my aunt gives me instructions
over the phone. I make a pot of spaghetti sauce, and the
Moosewood carrot soup I had, in a previous life, lived on
all winter. I ask Dina for recipes: six-cheese macaroni,
Brunswick stew.

And after a fashion, I ask my mother for help, too. After she died, I found three letters that she had written, during her first year of marriage, to her mother- and father-in-law. Now, I reread them. They are ebullient letters, vivacious and gracious and charming; they are everything best about her—her energy and her style and her hope. She wrote about concerts she and my father attended, and movies they saw. "We went to Durham for a Chinese dinner and then saw *My Fair Lady*," she wrote, and reading that letter in my bedroom in Durham, I wonder where exactly they ate, whether she drove past the house in which her daughter would one day live. In each of the letters, she is learning how to cook. She wrote about making coq au vin, corned beef, onion quiche. One night, she whipped cream until it turned to butter ("Dennis had to go out at 9:30 p.m. in search of more"); the first time she tried to make fondue, the fondue pot burst into flames. She describes these mishaps with a true writer's flair, with self-deprecation and humor, and I can picture her in that small kitchen with "the French cookbook" and her deter-mination to master a new thing. One Thursday, there was an especially disastrous pie. She didn't tell my grandpar-ents what kind of pie it was, only that the stiffly beaten egg whites sat too long and turned into a puddle; the yolks, meant to be warmed gently with a few other ingredients over medium heat, came out boiled. "Dennis wouldn't let me taste it until we served it—'who wants pie with a piece cut out?'" In the end, the pie turned out just fine: "Believe it or not everyone liked it. . . . I wouldn't have felt too badly if the recipe hadn't said 'EASY—even a novice cook can make this.'"

Her letters keep me company. As I fold and whisk, I think I sense my mother's shade. I think: *If she'd lived, maybe we could have gone on one of those culinary vacations, where you travel to some exotic spot and take a class in tempering chocolate or knife skills.* I think: *I am not as alone as I appear to be, here in my kitchen, trying to cook.*

In my mother's cookbooks, I mostly skip the quail and gazpacho and go to the chapters on bread and dessert. There is banana bread, orange cake, a recipe for cherry-walnut muffins next to which, some decades ago, she placed a check mark. I bake the muffins. I try out cheese bread, and overnight a blueberry crumb cake to a friend in New York. I bring oatmeal toffee cookies to a church committee meeting, and when people eat them, when people compliment them, it feels like George Eliot has called to tell me that she likes my books; it feels like the highest praise ever.

I find that I do most of this baking on Sunday afternoons. Sundays I come home from church and go to the kitchen and I bake tins of muffins, loaves of banana bread. Slowly, I begin to understand the timing, that all this Sunday afternoon baking is a response to church, that I want to feed people as Ellie feeds people, as I have been fed; not being a priest, all these muffins are the closest I can come. I read that bread is "regarded as necessary for sustaining life." I bake loaves of whole-wheat challah, zucchini bread. I leave them on doorsteps all over town.

middle tint

At the Cape Ann Museum in Gloucester, Massachusetts, looking at Fitz Lane's *The Western Shore with Norman's Woe*, an 1862 oil painting of a cove, water, a few clouds, a boat. It is distinguished by its palette, by what critics in the nineteenth century would have called middle tint— that is, the grays, the browns and blues and dull brick reds, not bright; the colors that do not sing out for your attention; the colors you might not notice if you are not looking for them. They are the gray curve of Lane's rocks, the enormous expanse of ochre sky. They are the putty of buildings that dominate a canvas but do not draw the eye. Middle tint makes the shadows in your painting; without it, your canvas would look flat. Standing here in this museum before Lane's great landscape, you might not linger on the middle tint, but without it, you would not be able to see the bright sharp clouds, the curve of stark black earth that holds your eye.

John Ruskin, the nineteenth-century art critic, said that the truly skilled painter devoted most of his canvas to middle tint. In a great landscape, there is "excessively small quantity, both of extreme light and extreme shade, all the mass of the picture being graduated and delicate middle tint. . . . The middle tint is laid before the dark colors, and before the lights." The painter should follow nature, said Ruskin; nature's landscapes are mostly all "middle tint, in which she will have as many gradations as you please" and only there in those miles of humble, sleeping green and brown does nature "touch her extreme lights, and extreme darks, isolated and sharp, so that the eye goes to them directly, and feels them to be key-notes of the whole composition."

Perhaps middle tint is the palette of faithfulness. Middle tint is going to church each week, opening the prayer book each day. This is rote, unshowy behavior, and you would not notice it if you weren't looking for it, but it is necessary; it is most of the canvas; it is the palette that makes possible the gashes of white, the outlines of black; it is indeed that by which the painting will succeed or fail. "Upon the strength of the middle tint depends, in a great measure, the general look of the picture," says one nineteenth-century handbook for aspiring artists. "The management of light and shade, as relates to a whole, ought to be always present in the student's mind, as it is from inattention to this alone that a work is often destroyed in its progress."

Maybe now in the middle, after the conversion, after ten years, on into twenty years, faithfulness is about recognizing that most of my hours will be devoted to painting the middle tint, the sky, the hillside on which no one will comment, the hillside that no one, really, will see. Maybe this is prayer most of the time, for most of my life; I will barely notice it; you will barely notice it; against this landscape of subtle grays, occasionally I will speak in tongues, occasionally I will hear an annunciation.

wall, again

I am talking to my spiritual director about the wall, how I
am noticing that the wall is not blank, how I have looked
at the wall long enough to see that what I first thought was
whitewash is actually opalescent, incandescent, like the
inside of a shell, like glazed porcelain. I tell her that now
I think I could stay here for forever, looking at the opales-
cence. Before she says it, I know what she will say: I cannot
stay here forever, any more than I could have stayed in
that conversion place. *Look again,* she says. *Pray the wall
again, and then look to your right, and you might see a
stairwell.*

failure, ii

> Loving God, it turns out, is hard precisely because
> it does not promise the reassuring logic of
> accomplishment and failure.
>
> —*Ryan Netzley*

From this place now—not in the midst of the marital
maelstrom; not in the middle of discovering God's abstraction, but a little while later—in this clearing, I can begin
to see those people and stories and words that held me to
something resembling the Christian faith; that hold me
still, if sometimes with a loose stitch.

It turns out the Christian story is a good story in which
to learn to fail. As the ethicist Samuel Wells has written,

some stories feature heroes and some stories feature saints and the difference between them matters: "Stories . . . told with . . . heroes at the centre of them . . . are told to laud the virtues of the heroes—for if the hero failed, all would be lost. By contrast, a saint can fail in a way that the hero can't, because the failure of the saint reveals the forgiveness and the new possibilities made in God, and the saint is just a small character in a story that's always fundamentally about God."

I am not a saint. I am, however, beginning to learn that I am a small character in a story that is always fundamentally about God.

rumors

I have heard that many of us sojourn in the middle for a long, long time; that we have many middles; that we keep meeting and making new middles. Maybe every ten years, like Ruth's mother said. Maybe, for some people, more often than that.

And I have heard that some people eventually leave the middle and arrive at an end. I have heard that this end is a place of wisdom, of beatitude. I have heard it is a place of unself-consciousness. I have heard there is a lot of give in the fabric there.

There is a woman I know in Arkansas. She is a minister's wife, and a minister in her own right, and she has a yoga studio in her backyard, and a piano decoupaged with old sheet music, and in her house is a door from every house she's ever lived in, and when she prays, I believe her, and she is the kind of Christian I hope one day to become. It is like the gospel and Jesus are so much in her that she doesn't have to worry about being a Christian anymore, she doesn't have to worry about it, she is just in that story and it is in her. At least, that's how it looks to me, from the outside. I'm sure she'd tell it differently, but that is how it looks to me.

I expect it takes a long time to get there.

metaphors

The Christian tradition is thick with metaphors for the
journey to God. The journey is like walking through a
castle. Inside the castle are seven rooms, some rooms
simple and spare, others full of alcoves and secret passage-
ways. In the first room, people are making a beginning
of humbly devoting themselves to God—they are turning
their attention to God, but they are still vulnerable, still
very much at risk of being pulled away. People in the
second room are increasingly able to hear God—through
holy conversation and holy reading, through prayer. In the
fourth room, you may begin to hear God's voice directly.
All the rooms are made of crystal, and they become more
and more suffused with light as you move closer to the
seventh room, which sits at the very center of the castle. In

this seventh room, all is light; in the seventh room is God.

Or the journey is like a ten-rung ladder of love. On the first rung the pursuer is sick with love, faint with love for God; on the third step the pursuer engages unfailingly in religious performances, in prayer, in acts of charity; by the seventh step her pursuit is characterized by her ardor, her boldness; on the tenth rung her soul is intertwined perfectly with God.

Or again, there is a mountain, swathed in darkness. The mountain is God, and the mountain is your movement toward God. This is what it is like to ascend to God: you are standing at the edge of an abyss, at the foot of a mountain that seems impassable.

All is soaked in darkness. You are fearful. Yet you want to go on.

author q & a

Lauren's friend, the editor and writer Mary Kenagy Mitchell (who heroically read many drafts of *Still*), asked Lauren a few questions about writing and spirituality.

You write about the difficulty of shaping middles, how we think of beginnings and ends as having all the drama and the middle just taking up space in between. What was it like to come up with a way to structure this book? Does it rise toward a crisis point, like a traditional drama, or does it do something different?

Structuring this book was hard. I wrote through about eight alternative structures before I finally settled on the fairly loose three-part structure. In one version, I was going to write a hundred short chapters, for Emily

Dickinson's believing and unbelieving a hundred times an hour. In another version, I set the entire book in the course of one day. I finally settled on this three-part structure because I wanted to emphasize the subtle but hugely significant shift from depressed, intense crisis to pacific openness, from no sense of God to a new sense of God. From wrenched and wrecked to calm communion with a God I both know and don't know. In part the structure was hard because what might be considered the real crisis point, to use your term, is the prelude to the book. The spiritual unraveling, the alienation from God that I felt after my mother's death and in the midst of my marriage—that is the backstory. *Still* opens at the tail end of that darkness. The book is not primarily a picture of the darkness. It is a picture of the end of the darkness, of the stumbling out of the darkness into something new.

The title, Still, *has several possible meanings, and its significance grows through the book. There's* still *as in "I'm still here," but also as in "Be still." Did you always have that title in mind? Were you "writing toward" it, and if so what was that like?*

I have a friend who is very practiced at meditation, and she sometimes speaks of being given a word for her meditating—being given a mantra, given a word. That is how I think of *still*. In general, I'm lousy at titling. This book is the first book I've written where I—and not the publisher—have chosen the title. But the word *still* simply came, and writing the book was in some ways nothing more and nothing less than writing my way into understanding what the word means for me. Originally, I thought I was writing a book that would answer the question, "Why are you still a Christian?" I would tell people that I was writing a book called *Still,* and they would laugh, saying that I was the least still person they knew.

As I wrote, new meanings of *still* emerged. For another project, I was reading around in volumes of Appalachian folklore, and of course there was a lot of folklore about moonshine. So I got to thinking about how you make moonshine. I got to thinking about distilling. In fact, in older usage, *still* was a verb that meant to distill: "We had plenty of roses; stilled some May 22," wrote a seventeenth-century minister named Ralph Josselin in his diary. And so of course I then got to thinking that this whole journey has been—is still—a process of distillation. That I am that rose, being distilled.

Later, I learned that *still* had a particular meaning in nautical idiom—that a still is the sound piped out by the boatswain's pipe to get the crew's attention and get them to stop working and stand at attention. And when I read that, I thought—God is that boatswain; there are moments I describe in this book that were precisely that, precisely about telling me to stop, to cease, to stand at attention. When a priest suggested that I'd lied the day of my wedding. When the friend I mention in the second chapter of the book shook me out of my self-pity by telling me that I should receive Ellie's hospitality as gift, as a response to my vulnerability, that my own vulnerability, maybe, was gift.

Also, most everything that's good about my writing is imitation. Some people are great creative geniuses, great artists; for those of us who are lesser, who are not great but who are trying to be good, one of the major things is figuring out what to imitate, what to copy. The title *Still* certainly owes something to Mary Karr's *Lit*—the one-syllable shortness, the double and more-than-double meaning.

In the book, you're in conversation with a lot of other writers, especially poets like Emily Dickinson and Anne Sexton. Does their poetry (or the work of other poets) influence your prose writing in any conscious way? How does that work?

As I was finishing *Still,* I read a book by Richard Rohr, *Falling Upward,* that described the spiritual life as having two halves. In the first half, a person is concerned with building an identity, with securing a self. This is the season in which a person builds a career, marries; and it is the season, religiously, in which a person is invested in securing a religious identity too. Rohr says that during the first half of a spiritual life, you are often concerned with engaging a religious institution, performing an established religious choreography. Then, he says, you have a crisis—there's a death or a flood, or you get divorced or you get fired. And then after the crisis, you might, if you embrace it, enter a second half of life—one in which you begin to hear "a deeper voice of God" than you heard before. "It will sound an awful lot like the voices of risk, of trust, of surrender, of soul, of 'common sense,' of destiny, of love, of an intimate stranger, of your deepest self." For obvious reasons, the trajectory Rohr sketched appeals to me (although I myself would not posit such a neat pattern of two halves severed by a crisis—maybe we move back and forth between the two halves; maybe there are seven halves). Anyway, here's the point: Rohr says that in the second half of your spiritual life you may find yourself reading a lot of poetry. Maybe, before, you read dogmatics or self-help how-tos or narrative history. Before, poetry may have seemed elusive and loopy. In the second of Rohr's two halves, you like the space that poetry offers. I read Rohr and thought it was no coincidence that most of what I'd been reading was poetry.

But you asked how reading poetry affects my writing. I love reading poems that have a lot of space—Deborah Digges's poems seem spacious to me, and Anna Kamienska's poems. When I read prose, especially when I read fiction, I am attracted to a very different kind of voice. One of my favorite novelists is Nancy Lemann. She writes about New Orleans, and the voice of her novels is New Orleans; Lemann flings words at her reader like confetti. The voice of her prose is not a spacious voice. It is a drunken voice, a voice of revelry, of circuits overloaded. I hope there is space in *Still*. Where there is space, it comes from my reading poems.

I am envious of poets, envious of their charge to pay attention to every single syllable. Of course, I, and I think most prose writers, try to attend to every syllable, every bit of rhythm, every phrase. My attention to those small units is informed, largely, by poetry. Also, I'm aware that there are several moments in *Still* that are very much playing with imagery, almost self-consciously influenced by the repetition and wordplay of poetry—for example, the long string of similes in the first chapter, a string that is meant in part to suggest precisely a narrator's groping to capture something she doesn't fully understand. Or the gingerbread cake's showing up as a symbol of brittleness in that same chapter, and then appearing in a quite different context, carrying quite different meaning in the chapter describing the May 15 Emily Dickinson celebration. I read poetry partly because I am drawn to that kind of playing with simile and image, and my own efforts at using such imagery and repetition here are clearly influenced by my diet of poetry. I leave it to the reader to decide whether those gestures toward poetic device work; they delight me, but a writer delighted by her own prose is a decidedly untrustworthy judge.

You also seem to spend a lot of time in museums. Why do the visual arts have such an appeal for you? Who are your favorites?

That's true—I can often be found in an art museum. Mostly I like being in a museum because I find visual art both absorbing and disorienting. I don't know very much about painting. I have taken exactly one art history course, and I can't draw a credible stick figure. I like being in a space where my senses are stimulated, indeed swamped, and where I don't know enough to think my way out of the experience. There's an analogy here to prayer. Every spiritual director I've ever had has tried to get me to pray without words: to pray in silence, or to pray by doodling, or to pray through dance. I think these wise people know that I am very comfortable with words, and that, given half a chance, I will think my way out of actually praying.

Speaking of spiritual directors, you write about your spiritual director in Still, *but you don't pause to explain what spiritual direction is or why you have a spiritual director.*

In general, I think that different people have different paths to God, different people are called to and nourished by different spiritual practices. That said, I don't think I've ever met the person who wouldn't benefit from spiritual direction. I think my spiritual life would have gone comatose long before now had it not been for the prodding, and the listening, of these generous directors. I think of spiritual direction as lending another set of ears to God's conversation with me. Or I think of it as analogous to my cello lessons, only instead of learning to play the cello, I am trying to learn to pray.

Did you write this book with a particular type of reader in mind, or do you not work that way?

I hope it does not sound too narcissistic to say that I wrote the book, first, for myself. I discover what I think by writing. Other people discover things in conversation, or by painting, or by taking solitary, reflective walks; but, as Harry Emerson Fosdick once said about himself, I think on paper. So, initially, I began writing because I needed to make sense of what happened in my spiritual life as and after my marriage ended. I understood that my spiritual life had largely withered during my marriage, and I understood that after a long dark period I had gotten somewhere new spiritually—I needed to map the contours of that for myself.

It sounds ridiculous to say this, but when I became a Christian—around age twenty-one—I didn't expect that my spiritual life would change much ever again. From this vantage point, that sounds so *naive,* but at the time, I thought "this conversion is a huge dramatic change, and then after this the course is set, and there just will be more and more of this." So when there *was* subsequent change— as of course there was and of course there will be—I needed a place to sort out those changes, and the place was a piece of paper, a laptop. Also my spiritual director's office, but foremost a piece of paper. As I began to write and to talk to other people about their spiritual lives, and to read with questions of spiritual stagnation and spiritual change at the forefront of my mind, I realized that many, many people come to a place where what they thought they knew about living the spiritual life doesn't quite match the actual life they're living. Sometimes that comes as a great crisis; sometimes it is slow and quiet. I hope that *Still*'s consideration of the moment when the grain of the spiritual life changes will connect with readers in their own very different moments of spiritual change.

In Still, *you mention that you are a historian, and that you teach at a divinity school. There are passing references to preaching. Why didn't you write more, or more straightforwardly, about your professional life—about the fact that you are the author of several books about spirituality, for instance?*

Good question. I went back and forth on this—how directly to name the ways that my professional and public life is imbricated with my faith—to what extent should I discuss the way my public religious life as a religious writer and divinity school professor conditioned my own experience of spiritual breakdown? To be sure, my experience of my mother's death was complicated by the fact that, before she died, I wrote a book with a chapter about grief, and my experience of divorcing was complicated by the fact that

I had written a book about chastity—about the ethics of intimacy—and here I was, patently failing in the realm of my own intimate relationship. And, to be sure, my experience of alienation from God was complicated in part by the fact that my job was to teach Christian spirituality to future pastors.

I can give you three explanations of why I chose to treat those complications more or less in passing in *Still*. First, I determined that it was not a falsifying omission—by which I mean, the truth of my experience, the heart of my experience, was not about my professional religious life, complicating as that was. The heart of the experience was somewhere else, somewhere more interior. When I wrote my way to that recognition, I felt I at least had the option of treating the public piece obliquely.

Then, second, I determined that the public, professional context of my own spiritual breakdown was a piece of my experience that wouldn't be shared by lots of readers. It would be shared, perhaps, by pastors who had a spiritual crisis, or other divorcing divinity school professors—but, back to your question about audience, it seems to me that the broader theme of *Still*—the simple fact of change, sometimes excruciating change, in one's spiritual life— would be relevant to a much broader audience than spiritually struggling pastors, and I didn't want to alienate those readers by going on and on about how weird it was to tell my divinity school dean that I might be getting a divorce.

But that is only a partial answer.

The rest of the answer is that it's still a very hard topic for me. It's still confusing and uncomfortable for me—that my divorce and my own spiritual crisis were to some extent inseparable from my life as a "professional Christian." So I didn't want to write about that imbrication, because it is too hard.

And yet—here I still am, carrying out my spiritual life in public, re-creating the context in which another future spiritual change may be inseparable from some public religious performance. I'm sure a therapist somewhere could tell you why I do this, dissect my spiritual life on the page for readers. I like to think I'm called to do it. My own spiritual life owes so much to reading, to books; I like to imagine my own books help other people, that they are a debt offering, a gratitude offering. Also, frankly, it is a kind of writing I enjoy—it is "deep play" for me, this kind of writing. Still, I don't think this book is really about me. If I've written it well, it isn't about me. It's about the questions: How does a spiritual life change? How do you enter that change?

So that may be related to something you write in the preface. The preface insists that Still *is not a memoir, but in many ways it reads like a memoir. What do you mean when you tell us it is not one?*

I'm making a fairly narrow point about genre there. I don't think this is a memoir because it's not really a narrative. I have forced the chapters into a sort of loose chronology, but more essentially, the chapters are discrete, thematically ordered reflections. I think of *Still* as an autobiographically inflected rumination on a focused spiritual theme—the theme of desolation and consolation. It is not storied enough to count, by my lights, as a memoir. As I read the book (and other people may read it differently—I don't think that my own reading is privileged), the narrative falls away over the course of the book. Part one is almost all narrative, almost all story. By part three, we are much closer to pure reflection. In a sense, that movement follows, formally, what I understood to be happening in my own spiritual life. In the crisis moments, I was desperate to narrate. As I moved somewhere else spiritually, out of crisis and into a new odd calm, I was more peaceably floating through whatever was happening. I wanted to record moments, but not so intently to tell stories.

I know that you read a lot of twentieth-century theology.
How did that reading influence your writing of this book?

While writing *Still*, I read a lot of theology of God's
absence. In general, the work that most compelled me was
by Jewish theologians whose wrestling with God's absence,
or God's hiddenness, was, in part, a response to the
Holocaust. The Holocaust makes questions about God's
hiddenness or absence imperative, and the canon of post-
Holocaust Jewish theology has an urgency about it, a seri-
ousness that commanded my attention. At the same time,
I found reading some of this work—Eliezer Berkovits,
David Wolpe—paralyzing. It brought me up short. Sitting
there reading about God's absence during a genocide—
well, my own feelings of God's absence in the midst of my
own small personal life seemed, frankly, petty. On the one
hand, I take individual people's spiritual lives—including
my own—very seriously. At the same time, when one is
reading *Hasidic Tales of the Holocaust,* this relentless focus
on my own personal, private struggles—oh woe is me, I
feel spiritually alone in my marriage, say—can seem a little
overwrought. I think both of those impulses are true—this
matters, this spiritual life, and we can only encounter God,
or not encounter God, in the life we have, even if it is a life
of bourgeois comfort, a life lived at the top of Maslow's

hierarchy of needs—well, that's my ridiculously privileged life, and I have to reckon with God inside that. On
the other hand it is also true that in the context of bracing
post–World War II Jewish theology, my own private angst
can seem disproportionate.

*You write about a visit to a writing class in a women's
prison that changed you. Did you ever go back there?*

I did. I am currently a regular faculty member in the
program that I mention in the chapter "Busyness During
Lent." If you had asked me after that first visit to name the
moment in my day—or even in my week, maybe my year—
when I felt most alive, most like I was where I should be,
doing what I should be doing—if you had asked when I
most felt the call of God, the nearness of God, I would have
said those two hours at the prison. So I left the prison that
night knowing I had to go back. In hindsight, it intrigues
me that my experience that night had to do with a subtle
transformation of time—from busyness to presence. One of
the logics of prison is a particular, distorting and distorted,
practice of time. Often, people describe the experience of
incarceration in terms of time—that time seems endless,
that time seems not to hold a past or a future. We have
the idiom "doing time," and that is just the point: in

incarcerating people, the state is taking their time from them—the state robs people of their control over time.

Still *is a book about middles—the middle of a spiritual life—and* Girl Meets God *was a book about a beginning. So that leaves endings. Can you imagine yourself eventually writing a book about the spirituality of late life, or a book about death?*

Perhaps! I hope that would be many years from now. Perhaps there might be other books to be written from moments in the middle? Or maybe I'll just be quiet for decades until I get closer to an end? Regardless of how I might frame other books, I suspect that spiritually there will be many more middles.

So what is next for you, spiritually, do you think?

I am very bad at predicting the future. Every time I have thought I had a handle on some plan for the future, it has turned out to be wrong. But with that caveat, there are a few things that seem to be before me, spiritually. I am in the ordination process in the Episcopal church. God willing, the bishop willing, the people consenting, I will be ordained soon. This is something I've wanted, thought about, discerned, desired, for many years—since before my baptism, even. I don't know how, exactly, ordination will change my spiritual life. In some ways, maybe it won't be so much a change as an intensification—not that priests have more intense spiritual lives than other people, but rather, for me, an intensification in that I will begin to inhabit a place in the church I have yearned to inhabit; I will be able to inhabit this office in the church that I've longed to inhabit for many years—so maybe less an intensification than a falling into place. A priest I know in Connecticut told me that it took her ten years— ten ordained years—until she really became a priest, ten years of living into priestly ordination. Second, theologically, I am still very much sorting through things pertaining to my divorce. Among other things, divorcing has shaken up the assumptions I bring to reading scripture. In leaving my marriage, I was doing something that was simply not permissible, not in the way I have always interpreted scripture, and that is something I remain troubled by, confused by—it is not something about which I feel cavalier. I don't know, as neatly as I once knew, what my hermeneutic of scripture is. What does it mean to be someone who affirms scripture's authority, someone who wants to live inside the scriptural story, but who has made a major life choice that contradicts something about which Jesus in the Gospels is pretty clear? I don't have a straightforward, stable answer to that. I expect I will be trying to work it out for a long time. And third, doodling prayer. Currently, doodling prayer is crucial to my spiritual life. Get *Praying in Color* by Sybil MacBeth if you want to know more. I am abiding with this God who feels elusive yet near. It is a good place to be.

acknowledgments

For criticism, encouragement, and many other gifts large and small, I am grateful to (and for):

Diana Butler Bass, Karin Bergquist, Molly Bosscher, Bill Brosend, Julie Burton, Jason Byassee, Cathie Caimano, Chuck Campbell, David Chappell, Brian Cole, Lil Copan, Linford Detweiler, Warren Farha, Jeanne Finan, Donna Freitas, David Fuquay, Paul Griffiths, Esther Hamori, Peter Hawkins, Richard Hays, Judith Heyhoe, Anne Hodges-Copple, Lynette Hull, Stevie Hull, Julia Kasdorf, Adrienne Koch, Carol Mann, Joel Marcus, Mickey Maudlin, Donyelle McCray, Erika Meitner, Mary Kenagy Mitchell, LaVonne Neff, Mark Oppenheimer, Stephanie Paulsell, Thea Portier-Young, Stephen Prothero, Suzanne Quist, Katy Renz, Mark Tauber, Barbara Brown Taylor, Leslie

Winner, Greg Wolfe, and the staff, faculty, and students of the Institute of Sacred Music, Yale University, especially director Martin Jean, and the students in my spring 2011 spiritual writing workshop—Brin Bon, Matthew Cortese, Rachel Duncan, Ashleigh Elser, Kimberly George, Rachel Heath, Lillian Jackman, Lisa Levy, Ashley Makar, Stephen Register, Rachel Sommer, and Jesse Zink.

Parts of "Pie Social" appeared in *A Spiritual Life: Perspectives from Poets, Prophets, and Preachers* edited by Alan Hugh Cole, Jr., and part of "Reading the Bible in Eight Places" appeared in *The Christian Century*.

Thank you.

notes

PREFACE

x   *a horse trainer named Buddy Crawford . . . "I don't remember the feeling all that well"* Jane Smiley, *Horse Heaven* (New York: Ballantine, 2000), 192–93.

xviii   *"Blessed assurance, Jesus is mine"* Fanny J. Crosby, "Blessed Assurance," in Kenneth W. Osbeck, *Amazing Grace: Illustrated Stories of Favorite Hymns* (Grand Rapids: Kregel, 1999), 12.

xviii   *"O Lord of melons, of mercy"* Mary Oliver, "On Thy Wondrous Works I Will Meditate," in Oliver, *Thirst* (Boston: Beacon, 2006), 59.

PART I EPIGRAPH

1   *"The truth is simpler"* Rowan Williams, "The Dark Night," in Williams, *A Ray of Darkness: Sermons and Reflections* (Cambridge, MA: Cowley, 1995), 81.

FAILURE

4   *their antecedents lay in medieval Saxony . . . and Ghana*
     On the heated scholarly debate about the origins of face
     jugs, see William C. Ketchum, "Jugs, Face," in Gerard C.
     Wertkin, ed., *Encyclopedia of American Folk Art* (New
     York: Routledge, 2004), 266; Charles C. Zug, *Turners
     and Burners: The Folk Potters of North Carolina* (Chapel
     Hill: Univ. of North Carolina Press, 1986), 382.

A POEM AT THANKSGIVING

12   *"Listen . . . dark though it is"* W. S. Merwin, "Thanks,"
     in Merwin, *Migration: New and Selected Poems* (Port
     Townsend, WA: Copper Canyon Press, 2005), 280.

ODE ON GOD'S ABSENCE

17   *"The Almighty and merciful Lord"* Book of Common
     Prayer (New York: Church Hymnal Corporation,
     1979), 321.

18   *"When the Word left me"* William Harmless, *Mystics* (New
     York: Oxford Univ. Press, 2008), 53.

18   *"It is not that I have a long journey . . . reality to my very
     self"* Rowan Williams, *Ponder These Things: Praying
     with Icons of the Virgin* (Brewster, MA: Paraclete, 2002),
     35–37.

20   *"He will shout with joy for you"* Zephaniah 3:17. This
     translation can be found at jbq.jewishbible.org/assets/
     Uploads/313/313_Silence2.pdf.

HEALING PRAYER

22   *"May God the Father bless you"* This is a slight modifi-
cation of a prayer found in the Book of Common Prayer,
460.

CHRISTMAS WITH ANNE SEXTON, DEAD POET

24   *"I am torn in two . . . it feels like thousands"* Anne Sexton,
"The Civil War," in Sexton, *The Complete Poems* (Boston:
Houghton Mifflin, 1981), 418–19.

24   *She wrote her last book* Anne Sexton and Gregory Fitz
Gerald, "The Choir from the Soul: A Conversation with
Anne Sexton," *The Massachusetts Review* 19, no. 1 (Spring
1978), 76–78.

24   *Her biographer says* Diane Wood Middlebrook, *Anne
Sexton: A Biography* (New York: Vintage Books, 1991),
368, 379–80. For a more sympathetic reading of Sexton's
late poems, see Alicia Ostriker, "Indecent Exposure?" in
The Women's Review of Books IX, 2 (November 1991), 4.

25   *Once, when she was in a mental hospital . . . "You pray for
me"* Sexton and Fitz Gerald, "The Choir from the Soul,"
76–78.

25   *"God dressed up . . . sing an anthem"* Sexton, "The Civil
War," 418–19.

26   *"she tells the sacred that it must answer to her private
experience of reality"* Alicia Ostriker, "That Story: The
Changes of Anne Sexton," in Steven E. Colburn, ed.,
Anne Sexton: Telling the Tale (Ann Arbor: Univ. of
Michigan Press, 1988), 282.

27   *"Oh angels . . . wide as an English bathtub"* Anne Sexton,

"Frenzy," in Sexton, *The Complete Poems* (Boston: Houghton Mifflin, 1981), 466–67.

PART II EPIGRAPH

29   *"Middles might be said"* Don Fowler, "Epic in the Middle of the Wood: *Mise en Abyme* in the Nisus and Euryalus Episode," in Alison Sharrock and Helen Morales, eds., *Intratextuality: Greek and Roman Textual Relations* (New York: Oxford Univ. Press, 2000), 109.

EPIPHANY

33   *"Yes, it is time to think about Christ again"* Anne Sexton to Brian Sweeney, November 24, 1970, in Linda Gray Sexton and Lois Ames, eds., *Anne Sexton: A Self-Portrait in Letters* (Boston: Houghton, 1991), 368.

34   *"Surely the darkness will cover me"* Psalm 139:10–11, Book of Common Prayer, 794.

35   *"This is my beloved Son, in whom I am well pleased"* Matthew 3:17, King James Version.

VISITS TO MY MOTHER'S GRAVE

41   *"What would I like about this if I liked it?"* "An Interview with Peter Schjeldahl," *Blackbird: An Online Journal of Literature and the Arts* 3, no. 1 (Spring 2004), http://www.blackbird.vcu.edu/v3n1/gallery/schjeldahl_p/interview_text.htm.

45   *The man who wrote "I Come to the Garden Alone" . . . that he was alive* Kenneth W. Osbeck, *101 Hymn Stories: The Inspiring True Stories Behind 101 Favorite Hymns* (Grand Rapids: Kregel, 1982), 123–24.

EXORCISM; BLESSING

47   *"Whole-house, deep cleaning"* Cheryl Mendelson, *Home Comforts* (New York: Scribner, 1999), 25.

50   *"The greatest among you"* Luke 22:26–27, NIV.

50   *"The cup of blessing"* 1 Corinthians 10:16, 31, NRSV.

51   *"Husbands, love your wives"* Ephesians 5:25–26, NIV.

51   *"We thank you, Almighty God"* Book of Common Prayer, 306.

51   *"until such time as I can pour"* A version of Rabbi Nachman of Breslov's prayer may be found in Jay Michaelson, *God in Your Body: Kabbalah, Mindfulness and Embodied Spiritual Practice* (Woodstock, VT: Jewish Lights, 2006), 164–65.

A THOUGHT, AFTER READING EMILY DICKINSON

53   *God has become illegible* Emily Dickinson, poem 820.

LONELINESS, I

55   *These desert people, Christians, left the cities . . . to find God in the rigors of the desert* There are many wonderful studies of the desert fathers. On the desert fathers' fleeing faith's fashionableness, see especially Gerald Sittser, *Water from a Deep Well: Christian Spirituality from Early Martyrs to Modern Missionaries* (Downers Grove: InterVarsity Press, 2007), 80–81.

55   *But there is one desert teaching . . . hunger is what the cave can teach* This is my embroidered retelling of a teaching and interpretation found in Simon Tugwell, *Ways of Imperfection: An Exploration of Christian Spirituality* (Springfield, IL: Templegate, 1985), 16.

LONELINESS, II

57   *"If you are afraid of loneliness"* John Auchard,
      "Introduction," in Auchard, ed., *The Portable Henry James*
      (New York: Penguin Classics, 2004), xxxiii.

MIDDLES

60   *"wasteland of our primary and secondary landscape," the
      "crack" between grammar school and high school* Quoted
      in Vincent A. Anfara, Jr., and Richard P. Lipka, "Relating
      the Middle School Concept to Student Achievement,"
      Middle School Journal 35, no. 1 (September 2003), 1.

60   *The Middle Ages are those centuries . . . wonders of
      today* Magne Sæbø, "The Problem of Periodization of
      the 'Middle Ages': Some Introductory Remarks," in
      Sæbø, ed., *Hebrew Bible Old Testament: The History
      of Its Interpretation* 1, part 2, *Middle Ages* (Gottingen:
      Vandenhoeck and Ruprecht, 2000), 23.

61   *middlestead* Paul Brassley, Anthony Lambert, and
      Philip Saunders, eds., *Accounts of the Reverend John
      Crakanthorp of Fowlmere 1682–1710* (Cambridge, U.K.:
      Cambridgeshire Records Society, 1988), 80.

62   *"His winnowing fork is in his hand"* Matthew 3:12, NIV.

PRAYER, LIVELY

64   *"Prayer . . . was not a skill at all"* Carrie Fountain,
      "Summer Practice," in *Burn Lake* (New York: Penguin,
      2010), 34.

66   *the first-century hermit . . . Archangel Michael* Glenn
      Peers, *Subtle Bodies: Representing Angels in Byzantium*
      (Berkeley: Univ. of California Press, 2001), 147–49.

66   *blessed Saint Radegund . . . even in her sleep* Jo Ann
McNamara and John E. Halborg with E. Gordon
Whatley, ed. and trans., *Sainted Women of the Dark Ages*
(Durham: Duke Univ. Press, 1992), 92.

67   *"Without prayer," Catherine Doherty once wrote* Catherine
Doherty, *Poustinia: Encountering God in Silence,
Solitude and Prayer* (Combermere, ON: Madonna House
Publications, 2000), 10.

PIE SOCIAL

73   *being well fed* My capacity to discern meaning and
fullness in this pie social owes much to conversations had
during the Evangelical Scholars of Christian Spirituality
gathering in 2009. I am grateful for the perspective those
conversations offered.

PRAYER, II

76   *I read a study . . . "Fairyland in the sky"* Diane Long,
David Elkind, and Bernard Spilka, "The Child's
Conception of Prayer," *Journal for the Scientific Study of
Religion* 6, no. 1 (Spring 1967), 101–9.

ANXIETY, I

80   *the truly anxious as well as some very skilled mere
worriers* On the distinction between anxious people and
worriers, see Patricia Pearson, *A Brief History of Anxiety:
Yours and Mine* (New York: Bloomsbury, 2008), 28–29.

82   *"self-examination and repentance"* Book of Common
Prayer, 265.

86   *"Her illness," Martin Luther wrote* Allan Hugh Cole, Jr., *Be Not Anxious: Pastoral Care of Disquieted Souls* (Grand Rapids: Eerdmans, 2008), 61.

ANXIETY, II

89   *The desert fathers ... sidle up alongside it and pray* Mary Margaret Funk, *Thoughts Matter: The Practice of the Spiritual Life* (New York: Continuum, 1998), especially 20–25. *On logismoi,* see also Roberta C. Bondi, *To Love as God Loves: Conversations with the Early Church* (Philadelphia: Fortress Press, 1987), 70–77.

90   *Francis de Sales ... "altogether quieted"* Cole, *Be Not Anxious,* 65–66; Francis de Sales, *Introduction to the Devout Life* (New York: Vintage, 2004), 203–4.

91   *"O God of peace"* Book of Common Prayer, 832.

91   *(Perhaps the refrain ... I'll be safe.)* On the ways that seemingly nonreassuring bedtime rituals—including scary fairy tales and lullabies that envision babies falling out of trees—give people a way to cope with anxiety, a "'recipe' for dealing with ... dread," see Pearson, *Brief History of Anxiety,* 24–28.

92   *"Be pleased, O LORD"* Psalm 40:13, NRSV.

92   *"pious formula[s] ... attacks of demons"* John Cassian, *Making Life a Prayer: Selected Writings of John Cassian* (Nashville: Upper Room Books, 1997), 55.

MANCHESTER PILGRIMAGE

94   *known for its architecture ... "Spinster of the Town of Manchester"* Stephen Roberts Holt, *Manchester-by-the-Sea* (Charleston, SC: Arcadia, 2009), 52–53; Jean

Strouse, *Alice James: A Biography* (Boston: Houghton Mifflin, 1980), 204, 311.

96   *Updike read Barth in his late twenties . . . his own undeniable longing* Jeff Campbell, "Interview with John Updike," in James Plath, ed., *Conversations with John Updike* (Oxford: Univ. Press of Mississippi, 1994), 102; Katherine Stephen, "John Updike Still Finds Things to Say About Life, Sex, and Religion," in Plath, ed., *Conversations*, 187; "Barth, Karl," in Jack De Bellis, *The John Updike Encyclopedia* (Westport: Greenwood Press, 2000), 47–49; Donald J. Greiner, "Body and Soul: John Updike and *The Scarlet Letter*," *Journal of Modern Literature*, 15, no. 4 (Spring 1989), 475–95, especially 488.

98   *God gives us many gifts, but "God is He Who gives God"* Augustine, *On the Trinity*, XV.26.46; see also "A Discussion Between Jacques Derrida and Jean-Luc Marion," in John D. Caputo and Michael J. Scanlon, eds., *God, the Gift, and Postmodernism* (Bloomington: Indiana Univ. Press, 1990), 55.

98   *"generally comforting and pleasant"* Campbell, "Interview with John Updike," 103.

ACROSS THE STREET FROM THE DICKINSON HOUSE

99   *"Largest Lover . . . prepare the way for another"* These images of Jesus are drawn from Dickinson's poems 573, 1487, 971, 567, 553, 1492, 1612, 1123, 357, and 698. My reading of Dickinson's Jesus draws heavily on Dorothy Huff Oberhaus, " 'Tender Pioneer': Emily Dickinson's Poems on the Life of Christ," *American Literature* 59, no. 3 (October 1987), 341–58. It is Oberhaus

who calls attention to Webster's 1844 definitions of "tender" and "pioneer," and who explains the concept of "kenning." I also rely on Jane Donahue Eberwein, *Dickinson: Strategies of Limitation* (Amherst: Univ. of Massachusetts Press, 1985), 248–53; James McIntosh, *Nimble Believing: Dickinson and the Unknown* (Ann Arbor: Univ. of Michigan Press, 2000), 110–21; Rowena Revis Jones, "A Taste for 'Poison': Dickinson's Departure from Orthodoxy," *The Emily Dickinson Journal*, 2, no. 1 (Spring 1993), 47–64; Roseanne Hoefel, "Emily Dickinson Fleshing Out a New Word," *The Emily Dickinson Journal*, 1, no. 1 (Spring 1992), 54–75; and Roger Lundin, *Emily Dickinson and the Art of Belief* (Grand Rapids: Eerdmans, 1998), especially 177–78.

WISDOM FROM MY FRIEND S., WHICH IS SOMETHING OF A COMFORT

102 *she feels God is there for her ... "effortlessly"* "S."—Stanley Hauerwas—has expressed this sentiment (to me and to others) numerous times. For one iteration, see "Hannah's Child: Stanley Hauerwas on 'Becoming Christian,'" *Divinity* 10, no. 1 (Fall 2010), 17.

BUSYNESS DURING LENT

103 *"I thought about sloth"* Saul Bellow, *Humboldt's Gift* (New York: Penguin Books, 1996), 306.

104 *"busyness is the new sloth"* Geraldine is not the only person to have made this connection. *Inter alios*, a colleague linked business and laziness or sloth in conversation with me in the late 1990s. See also Rebecca

Konyndyk DeYoung, *Glittering Vices: A New Look at the Seven Deadly Sins and Their Remedies* (Grand Rapids: Brazos Press, 2009), 82–97; and Eugene H. Peterson, *The Contemplative Pastor: Returning to the Art of Spiritual Direction* (Grand Rapids: Eerdmans, 1989), 18; and Frederick Buechner, *Beyond Words: Daily Readings in the ABC's of Faith* (San Francisco: HarperOne, 2004), 371.

106 *In 1769 . . . barred from his own pulpit* Rhys Isaac, *Landon Carter's Uneasy Kingdom: Revolution and Rebellion on a Virginia Plantation* (New York: Oxford Univ. Press, 2004), 249.

108 *"You only need a tiny scrap of time"* Anonymous, *The Cloud of Unknowing,* ed. Bernard Bangley (Brewster, MA: Paraclete, 2006), 7.

PURIM

110 *"wine was served"* Esther 1:7, NIV.

110 *"There is a certain people"* Esther 3:8–9, NIV.

111 *On Purim . . . drown out Haman's name* Arthur Waskow, *Seasons of Our Joy: A Modern Guide to the Jewish Holidays* (Boston: Beacon, 1982), 125–26.

113 *"Esther did not reveal"* Esther 2:10, NRSV.

113 *"I will surely hide my face"* Deuteronomy 31:18, NRSV. For discussions of the theme of hiddenness in Esther, see (among many other sources that treat Esther and hiddenness) Timothy K. Beal, *Esther* (Collegeville: Liturgical Press, 1999), xx–xxi; Timothy K. Beal, *The Book of Hiding: Gender, Ethnicity, Annihilation, and Esther* (New York: Routledge, 1997); Avivah Zornberg, *The*

Murmuring Deep: Reflections on the Biblical Unconscious
(New York: Schocken, 2009), 108–9.

AFTER PURIM, THE EUCHARIST

116   *something St. Francis of Assisi wrote* Regis J. Armstrong,
ed., *Francis and Clare: The Complete Writings* (Mahwah,
NJ: Paulist, 1982), 58.

THE FEAST OF ST. JOSEPH

119   *"drive away all sickness . . . be found by God"* Book of
Common Prayer, 456, 386.

ANOTHER GOOD REASON TO GO TO CHURCH

120   *In the Sunday* Washington Post . . . *"off I went to church"*
V. C. Chickering, "Church Junkie," *Washington Post,* April
26, 2009; Jason Byassee, *The Gifts of the Small Church*
(Nashville: Abingdon, 2001), 43, n. 3.

BOREDOM

123   *The word* boredom . . . *"trivialize the world"* Patricia
Meyer Spacks, *Boredom: The Literary History of a State
of Mind* (Chicago: Univ. of Chicago Press, 1996), 12–14.

124   *Educational theorists have developed . . . "resistance
to . . . authority"* Reed W. Larson and Maryse H.
Richards, "Boredom in the Middle School Years: Blaming
Schools Versus Blaming Students," *American Journal of
Education* 99, no. 4 (August 1991), 418–43.

126   *"Gradually . . . a sense of order"* Monica Furlong,
"Alienation and Solitude" [talk given at the Merton

Conference in Winchester, U.K., December 1993], www
.thomasmertonsociety.org/furlong.htm.

IN BOSTON, THEOLOGY FOR THE MIDDLE

129 *"I call myself a Christian"* John Updike, "Introduction," to
F. J. Sheed, ed., *Soundings in Satanism* (New York: Sheed
and Ward, 1972), xi.

130 *Pike was an Episcopal bishop . . . "simply can't be 'prosy'
about."* James A. Pike, "The Three-Pronged Synthesis,"
Christian Century, December 21, 1960, 1496–1500;
David M. Robertson, *A Passionate Pilgrim: A Biography
of Bishop James A. Pike* (New York: Knopf, 2004), especially 108–13, 178–80; "Spiritualism: Search for a Dead
Son," *Time,* May 15, 1968.

READING THE BIBLE IN EIGHT PLACES

134 *"strengthening the nation's capacity . . . protect public
safety"* U.S. Immigration and Customs Enforcement
news release, March 25, 2010, http://www.ice.gov/news/
releases/1003/100325phoenix.htm.

135 *"Love is patient; love is kind"* 1 Corinthians 13:4, 7–8,
NRSV.

136 *dislocated exegesis* Stanley P. Saunders and Charles
L. Campbell, *The Word on the Street: Performing
the Scriptures in the Urban Context* (Grand Rapids:
Eerdmans, 2000), 90–94.

137 *"Do not worry . . . knows that you need [these things]"*
Matthew 6:25–26, 31–32, NIV.

137 *eagles' wings* See Isaiah 40:31.

137   *"And he saith unto me"* Revelation 19:9, KJV.

138   *"became clean like that of a young boy"* 2 Kings 5:14, NIV.

138   *tower of Babel* See Genesis 11:1–9.

138   *"for fear of the Jews"* John 20:19, NRSV.

139   *My researches uncover the following . . . are blank* CliffsNotes on Nicholas Sparks' A Walk to Remember, *Teacher's Guide,* (Hoboken, NJ: Wiley, 2009), 52; *The Sacred Hoop* [adapted from the play *Black Elk Speaks* by Christopher Sergel and based on the book *Black Elk Speaks* by John G. Neihardt] (Woodstock, IL: Dramatic Publishing, 1995), 24; Herman Lebovics, *Bringing the Empire Back Home: France in the Global Age* (Durham, NC: Duke Univ. Press, 2004), 96; Alicia Suskin Ostriker, "A Triple Hermeneutic: Scripture and Revisionist Women's Poetry," in Athalya Brenner and Carole Fontaine, eds., *A Feminist Companion to Reading the Bible: Approaches, Methods and Strategies* (Chicago: Sheffield Academic Press, 1997), 80–81.

141   *lonely places to pray* Luke 5:16, NIV.

HOLY SATURDAY VISITATION

146   *"Is there anything about loss"* Nicola Slee, "The Losses of Mary," in Slee, *The Book of Mary* (Harrisburg, PA: Morehouse, 2007), 100.

EASTER VIGIL

147   *"The hand of the LORD . . . a vast multitude"* Ezekiel 37:1–10, NRSV.

AFTER A LECTURE ABOUT JEWISH-CHRISTIAN METAPHORS

150 *why I am not wild about the metaphor of Christianity's having Jewish roots* As New Testament scholar Amy-Jill Levine has noted, although we often speak about Judaism and Christianity as having a parent-child relationship, it may be more accurate to speak of them as siblings, struggling over the question of who has been faithful to their shared parent (the God of Israel). See Amy-Jill Levine, *The Misunderstood Jew: The Church and the Scandal of the Jewish Jesus* (San Francisco: Harper San Francisco, 2006), 5. This may be an especially apt correction insofar as often, when people speak of Christianity's having Jewish roots, or of Christianity's being the daughter of Judaism, what people imagine as "Judaism" is rabbinic Judaism, which emerged in tandem with Christianity. Furthermore, the sibling metaphor is helpful because it does not suggest—as might "roots" or "parent-daughter"— that the younger, newer religion has somehow supplanted or replaced its forebear. See also Alan F. Segal, *Rebecca's Children: Judaism and Christianity in the Roman World* (Cambridge: Harvard Univ. Press, 1986).

PART III EPIGRAPH

151 *"A gray, gray day"* Anna Kamienska, "The Notebook, 1973–1979," in Kamienska, *Astonishments: Selected Poems of Anna Kamienska*, ed. and trans. by Grażyna Drabik and David Curzon (Brewster, MA: Paraclete Press, 2008), 124.

TWO CONVERSATIONS

153 *Then Jesus turned to the Twelve* John 6:67–68, NLT.

MIDDLE VOICE

155 *Linguists say it is hard . . . (washing one's hands)*
Suzanne Kemmer, *The Middle Voice* (Amsterdam:
Benjamins, 1993), especially 15–24.

EUCHARIST, III

158 *Taste and see that the Lord is sweet* Rachel Fulton, "'Taste
and See That the Lord Is Sweet' (Ps. 33:9): The Flavor of
God in the Monastic West," *The Journal of Religion* 86,
no. 2 (April 2006), 181–82.

Most English Bibles render this line as "taste and see
that the Lord is good." Fulton offers (among many other
insights) a fascinating account of various translators'
handlings of the Hebrew *tov*—whose primary meaning
is *good* but can also mean *sweet*. Those who translated
the psalm into Latin disagreed among themselves:
some translators rendered *tov* as *suavis* (sweet), others
(including Jerome) as *bonus* (good). Most English trans-
lations have followed Jerome's pattern—thus the tendency
of English-speaking Christians to think of the verse as
"taste and see that the Lord is good." Fulton, leaning on
Augustine, makes a compelling case for instead speaking
of the Lord's sweetness.

159 *The psalmist wrote about God's sweetness . . . "Drink
the sweetness"* Fulton, "'Taste and See That the Lord Is
Sweet,'" 169–204.

FEMALE SAINTS, THEIR INTIMACY WITH JESUS

160   *"I am set afire"* Margaret Ebner in Leonard Patrick
Hindsley, ed., *Margaret Ebner: Major Works* (Mahwah,
NJ: Paulist, 1993), 57.

160   *"Our Savior is our true Mother"* Julian of Norwich in
Edmund Colledge and James Walsh, eds., *Showings*
(Mahwah, NJ: Paulist, 1978), 292.

160   *"O my beloved Christ"* Elizabeth of the Trinity in
Jennifer Wild, ed., *The Westminster Collection of Christian Meditations* (Louisville: Westminster John Knox,
2000), 119.

160   *"We are so fastened"* Katherine of Alexandria in
Anne Savage and Nicholas Watson, eds., *Anchoritic
Spirituality: Ancrene Wisse and Associated Works*
(Mahwah, NJ: Paulist, 1991), 275.

LECTURE ABOUT LIGHT

164   *"the light of the world"* John 8:12, KJV.

164   *"like a great ring"* Henry Vaughn, "The World (I)," in Jay
Parini, ed., *The Wadsworth Anthology of Poetry* (Boston:
Thomson Wadsworth, 2006), 1251.

164   *"the light of the righteous"* Proverbs 13:9, KJV.

164   *"no light"* Milton, *Paradise Lost*, bk. 1, line 62.

EMILY DICKINSON, MAY 15

166   *consonant rhyme and eye-rhyme* Cynthia Griffin Wolff,
Emily Dickinson (Cambridge, MA: Da Capo Press, 1988),
186.

166   *"On subjects of which we know nothing"* Emily Dickinson,
The Letters of Emily Dickinson, ed. Thomas H. Johnson

and Theodora Ward (Cambridge, MA: Harvard Univ. Press, 1958), 3:728. Insightful discussions of this passage include Lundin, *Emily Dickinson and the Art of Belief*, especially 3, 140; Roger Lundin, *Believing Again: Doubt and Faith in a Secular Age* (Grand Rapids: Eerdmans, 2009), 115; McIntosh, *Nimble Believing*, especially 1–3; and Kathleen Norris, *Acedia and Me: Marriage, Monks, and a Writer's Life* (New York: Riverhead, 2008), 83. See also Norris's May 15 commemoration of Emily Dickinson in Norris, *The Cloister Walk* (New York: Riverhead, 1997), 221–22. My own commemoration of Dickinson is gratefully inspired by Norris.

TERMINOLOGY

168 *"Mental acceptance" Oxford English Dictionary*, 2nd ed., s.v. "belief," 2nd definition.

169 *"Faith . . . meant more than intellectual assent"* Christopher Grasso, "Skepticism and Faith," *Commonplace: The Interactive Journal of Early American Life* 9, no. 2 (January 2009), http://www.common-place.org/vol-09/no-02/grasso/.

CONFIRMATION

170 *I have always been a little fuzzy . . . placed on your head* My thinking about confirmation is influenced by James F. Turrell, "Muddying the Waters of Baptism: The Theology Committee's Report on Baptism, Confirmation, and Christian Formation," *Anglican Theological Review* 88 (2006), 341–59.

THINGS ELLIE SAYS IN CHURCH

173   *make the world into the Eucharist* Samuel Wells, *God's Companions: Reimagining Christian Ethics* (Malden, MA: Blackwell, 2006), 215–23.

A SUNDAY MORNING IN MASSACHUSETTS

175   *"If Christ is to visit us"* Elena Shvartz, "A Gray Day," trans. Stephanie Sandler, *Poetry* 198, no. 3 (June 2011), 237–38.

AFTER THE EUCHARIST, BAKING

188   *"regarded as necessary for sustaining life"* Rose Levy Beranbaum, *The Bread Bible* (New York: W. W. Norton, 2003), 543.

MIDDLE TINT

190   *"excessively small quantity . . . key-notes of the whole composition"* John Ruskin, *Modern Painters* (London: Smith, Elder, 1848), 1:179–80.

190   *"Upon the strength . . . destroyed in its progress"* John Burnet, *Practical Essays on Art*, ed. Edward L. Wilson (New York: Edward L. Wilson, Publisher, 1888), 38.

FAILURE, II

193   *"Loving God, it turns out"* Ryan Netzley, *Reading, Desire, and the Eucharist in Early Modern Religious Poetry* (Toronto: Univ. of Toronto Press, 2011), 20.

194   *"Stories . . . told with . . . heroes"* Stanley Hauerwas and Samuel Wells, "Theological Ethics," in Rupert Shortt, ed., *God's Advocates: Christian Thinkers in Conversation* (Grand Rapids: Eerdmans, 2005), 180.

RUMORS

196   *I expect it takes a long time to get there* This chapter is a
        grateful riff on a passage by Jane Smiley. In her novella
        The Age of Grief, the narrator, Dave Hurst, describes that
        titular age and then says, "I understand that later you
        come to an age of hope, or at least resignation. I suspect
        it takes a long time to get there." Smiley, *The Age of Grief*
        (New York: Anchor Books, 1987), 132.

METAPHORS

197   *a castle . . . a ten-rung ladder . . . a mountain* These
        images are drawn (and adapted) from Teresa of Avila,
        The Interior Castle (my summary of which is especially
        indebted to Mary Frohlich's account in Arthur Holder,
        ed., *Christian Spirituality: The Classics* [New York:
        Routledge, 2010], 211–16); John of the Cross, *Dark Night
        of the Soul;* and Gregory of Nyssa, *The Life of Moses.*

author's note

For various reasons—some personal, some literary—I have changed names and identifying details of people and institutions; I have sometimes modified chronology, and some of the minor characters are composites.

credits